the simple guide to DOG TRAINING

Tom Philbin

T.F.H. Publications, Inc.

Contents

The Basic Command Page 157-163

Home Alone
Page 178

Part Four: Advanced Training

Chapter 12: Trick Training

Part One
Choosing Your Dog

"You know Sam, I'm beginning to suspect ol' Fifi here just isn't the dog for me."

Introduction

Why train your dog? Why not just take care of the dog's physical, medical, and emotional needs, and let it go at that? The answer is control. No matter what breed of dog you own, the dog's life, your life, and the rest of your family's lives will be easier with a trained dog. For example, when you take your trained dog out for a nice walk, he won't bolt after the nearest garbage truck or start a mad dash after the neighbor's cat across a four-lane road. You will bark, as it were, "Stay," and he will stop because you have anticipated his inborn reaction to a situation and are primed to issue a command that he will understand and obey.

A trained dog may not fight with other dogs, and—this is not insignificant—he won't use your house as a

A well-trained dog is a pleasure to own.

bathroom or your favorite ottoman as a chew toy. What's more, you'll enjoy the dog, because you and he will be happier and have more opportunities to have a good time with one another.

Various types of training are covered in this book, and the assumption is that readers have no previous experience in dog training. As such, the "how to" strives to be as detailed and as basic as possible. It covers housetraining; simple obedience commands, such as sit and stay; off-leash commands; and tricks, such as jumping and crawling. It may not make your dog a Hollywood star, but it certainly will make him a star in your own home. It also tells you how to turn your dog into a Canine Good Citizen® and offers tips and hints on what's involved in getting your dog to participate in a variety of dog sports and take on special jobs, such as search and rescue, therapy work, and, of course, dog shows.

Why would you want to change a trait? One trainer/breeder I know, Linda Rudolph of Des Moines, Iowa, breeds Flat-Coated Retrievers. Their main instinct, as the name suggests, is to retrieve things. "Every day," Linda says, "My dogs retrieve my shoes or slippers." Linda doesn't find this annoying; she finds it cute—and natural.

But before training, you must know what dog is right for you and your family, particularly if you have small children. There are over 200 varieties of dog and while all share similar characteristics because they have a common ancestor—the wolf—all are different in some way, sometimes vastly different.

Dogs come in a variety of shapes, sizes, and colors and have different instincts or traits that mandate different treatment. For example, dogs in the Hound Group are used for tracking, and, in the absence of someone to track, they have to be exercised every day. If they're not, they can become bored and destructive and may suffer from other behavior problems—just as you would if you were used to sailing ships and suddenly were confined to a small room doing crossword puzzles. Other dogs don't care a whit about exercise and will hang around the house all day with no problem at all.

Because of these differences, a comprehensive capsule guide to the dog breeds is presented, and the accent is on honesty. If a dog has some behavior problems, is difficult to train or housetrain, or is like a whirling dervish around the house, this information is explained in detail. It would be unfair to do otherwise. The facts, as I see them, are presented. It is up to the individual to make a decision as to whether he wants a particular dog after getting the whole story—good and bad. Training can only go so far. You cannot completely control the inborn traits of your dog, but you can often control the results.

This book also contains a general chapter that discusses other factors involved in selecting a dog, such as sex, life span, cost, grooming, and includes a very important factor–where to get your dog. Not all places are equal–far from it. Some are downright unethical, if not immoral and criminal, the chief sin being overbreeding dogs without regard to their health or well-being. The result is that dogs are sold that are very poor examples of a breed or that have undesirable qualities, such as shyness or aggression.

Health matters are also covered in detail. Health information can help you in a number of ways. First, it will enable you to take care of your pet when he is sick and to recognize symptoms of various maladies when they first occur. Additionally, it will enable you to select a dog with full knowledge of the breed's potential health problems. For example, certain large-eyed breeds, such as Pugs and Pekingese, are more susceptible to having their eyes easily damaged.

There is also a chapter on understanding the mental processes of a dog, because it's always good to know the psychological underpinning of various training techniques. You can train with greater confidence and fine-tune the training sessions based on this basic understanding. Sprinkled throughout the book are facts that will help you with training, help you to understand dogs better, or help you to keep your sense of humor.

Special note should be made, I think, of the summaries of key points after each of the chapters. These can be helpful in getting a quick idea of the particular information that you should be absorbing, as well as alerting you to what information is contained in a chapter if more details are wanted.

It seems clear that a variety of methods can be used in training a dog. Some people favor positive reinforcement, others feel that saying the word "No" is fine when it comes to training, and others can be even firmer. I think that the key in training your dog is to use techniques that you can live with. If you find an approach uncomfortable, there's no point to using it. You're not going to able to use it effectively.

This book approaches dogs as if they were human beings. Of course, dogs are different than people, but the fundamental foundation is mindful that dogs have feelings and they are living creatures that deserve respect and love. Maybe that's the main point to remember. Dogs thrive on affection, and if they share one universal characteristic, it is that they want to please their masters. For training to be effective, love really must be a two-way street.

Choosing a Dog

Most people pick a dog according to his appearance, but this is risky. Indeed, you should approach getting a dog with the same fervor and comprehensiveness that you might exert in adopting a child, because in a very real sense, that's just what you are doing. Choose the wrong one and your experience can be unhappy, both for you and the dog.

I had one such unhappy experience. When my children were young and we were inexperienced in the ways of dogs, we bought an Irish Setter for them just because he was beautiful and the breed had a good reputation with kids. What I did not know was that it was a difficult breed to train—very difficult. It was October when I bought the dog from a

A mixed breed can offer just as much love as a purebred.

Questions to Ask Before Getting a Dog

- How long will he live?
- What are his breed characteristics (aggressive; tendency to dig, roam, bark, seek water; nervous; destructive; difficult to train; difficult to housetrain; temperament)?
- What is the dog's personality now?
- Can I afford to care for him?
- Does the breed have health concerns?
- What is his activity level?
- What size will he grow to as an adult?
- What are his parents like?

"breeder" (though I had no idea that they could vary greatly in quality) and dubbed him "Rusty." Then the winter came. I remember that winter very well, walking Rusty through frigid temperatures for 45 minutes or more at a time, and trying, coaxing, begging, and, finally, praying to get him to do his business. He did–immediately upon getting back inside the house.

In desperation, we sent Rusty to a professional trainer. The pro was unsuccessful, and I ended up giving Rusty away to a farmer. At his new home, he could roam outside for hours in the fields and where he did his business was not an issue. But my children, grown now, still remember Rusty with affection and regret–and so do I.

Mixed Breeds Versus Purebreds

There are a number of factors to consider before getting a dog, and one decision is whether to get a mixed-breed dog or a purebred. A purebred dog can be defined as having a mother and father of the same breed, as well as a number of generations of the same breed before them.

Fascinating Facts

- Americans spend ten billion dollars a year taking care of their dogs and cats, and most of that money is spent on food.
- There are more different types of dog than any other animal in the world.
- The smaller the dog, the faster he matures.
- Puppies are deaf until they're around 20 days old.
- Dogs with curly coats, like Poodles, don't shed hair.
- Blonde bombshell actress Jean Harlow named her dog "Oscar" so that she could always say she had gotten one.
- St. Patrick, who, as a young man, had been kidnapped from his native England, escaped from Ireland by hiding himself among a shipload of Irish Wolfhounds bound for England.
- Dogs have been around man for a long time. Remains found in the Yukon have been carbon-dated to be 20,000 years old.

There are a couple of advantages to getting a mixed breed, one of which is a better health record. Purebred dogs may have some inherited medical problems, which can get expensive both fiscally and emotionally. A mixed breed or "mutt," on the other hand, is classically healthier, perhaps because undesirable maladies have fallen by the wayside as it was bred over the years, leaving only the healthier strains. Another advantage is that a mixed-breed dog is a lot cheaper than a purebred dog. Many people will give a mixed breed away for free, and shelters and humane societies charge a considerably lesser fee than breeders.

However, when you buy a purebred dog–assuming you're getting a good example of the breed–you can more or less predict what the dog will be like (and won't be like) when he is fully grown. For example, if you want a dog that's great with kids, choose a Basset Hound; if you want one that is extremely smart, get a Poodle; or if you want one that's a good retriever, get a Labrador. These predictions may not be possible if you buy a mixed-breed puppy that looks like his Beagle mother but acts more like his German Shepherd father.

Background Check

Whether purebred or mixed breed, you should try to find out as much as you can about the dog's background; not only his parents but, if he is an adult, where he came from. Was he abused? Does he dislike men, women, or children?

One experienced dog trainer says he once made a mistake with a 70-pound male Chow Chow. He didn't ask enough questions, and before he knew it, the dog had launched a full-scale attack on him. Only his experience saved him from serious harm, though he was bitten. He said that the person who supplied the dog neglected to tell him a little fact—the dog hated men.

Dog trainer and breeder Linda Rudolph says that "when you look at the mutt, try to surmise what are its dominant features." For example, if he looks a lot like a Poodle, he may grow up with Poodle-like characteristics. Also, his personality may be very similar to the purebred dogs in his background.

Size

In terms of size, dogs vary much more than people. The difference between the large-sized dog and the small-sized dog is immense, with a large dog weighing 30 or 40 times what a small one weighs.

One question to ask yourself is: How big of a dog can you comfortably handle, not only in terms of walking and playing with him, but in terms of living space? If you are a frail, elderly person, you might want to think twice before you buy an Irish Wolfhound. If you

Choose your dog carefully.

have a small apartment, you may not want to have a Great Dane or other large breed. Despite the fact that Great Danes and other large breeds are relatively inactive, they can still take up a lot of space and get in your way. Also, at some point you may want to travel, and a large dog is going to be more of a problem than a Chihuahua.

Male or Female?

When it comes to dogs, males are from Mars and females are from Venus. Even if they have been neutered, males tend to be more aggressive than females and will have a general tendency to roam and get into more fights with other dogs than females. Females are much more even-tempered.

On the negative side, females do come into heat twice a year and will spray a urine-scented substance that's not pleasant (unless you're a male dog), inviting every male dog in the neighborhood to come and visit. Also, females tend to be more excitable than males and tend to spontaneously urinate more readily. They can also be harder to housetrain.

Males and females make equally good pets.

Females are generally more patient and caring with their owner's children than males, while males are more protective of the family than females. Males are also bigger, of course. In the larger breeds, a male may weigh as much as 40 pounds more than a female.

Dog breeding should be left to the professional breeders who have the time, experience, and knowledge to invest in furthering the breed. Pet owners should not breed their dogs. Instead, they should have their pet neutered or spayed. This simple operation calms sex urges, eliminates spraying, and, in general, creates a more quiescent pet. Spaying or neutering also helps prevent certain cancers of the reproductive organs.

Part 1

Can't We All Just Get Along?

While an argument could be made that dogs are the most huggable, lovable creatures anywhere, Jean Craighead George reminds us in her in her book, *How To Make Your Dog Talk*, that they are "descended from wolves" and have instincts and needs, as well as pack rules and regulations. It's important that these are observed when bringing a new dog or dogs into your household.

If you want to have two dogs, your best bet is to bring them into the household together. They should be treated equally and given different eating bowls and eating places. If you have a choice, by all means bring in dogs that are neutered and of opposite sexes. They will generally get along best.

The closer the dogs are in terms of age, the larger the possibility that there will be some infighting. To eschew this, some vets advise that you bring in either a dog that is a couple of years older or younger than the resident pooch.

If one dog is a lot older than the other dog, the younger pooch may try to establish himself as the top dog, or "alpha," and reduce the older dog to the "omega," or bottom member of the pack. Says George: "This is something that a dog owner may notice when he introduces a brash young dog into a family in which there is also an aging pet. The young one may challenge the older dog's position—chase it from its food, take over its favorite sleeping spot, push it for more affection—and then the old dog's status falls. The dog is noticeably depressed: head and tail droop, the ears are held low. Like the old family dog, an older wolf may give up its position. An aged alpha in Mount McKinley Park walked off and left his pack when challenged by a young leader. A 'lone wolf,' he roamed the forest living off small game until he died several months later."

Activity Level

Dog trainer Captain Haggerty believes that a dog's activity level should be one of the most important factors in the selection process. If a dog has a high-activity level, hops all around the house, jumps up on things, and never seems to relax when confined, it can be disconcerting. If a dog is prone to barking, such as a Jack Russell Terrier (one owner we know characterizes the breed as "Jack Russell Terrorists"), this can be annoying as well.

Time

Another factor to consider in the selection process is the amount of time you have to devote to a dog. You may work a lot and have limited time, and some breeds, such as hunting dogs, like wide-open spaces and lots of exercise. Over the years, this dog may do fine in an apartment, but it's not really fair to keep a dog cooped up when he yearns to be free. If you

Active dogs need active owners.

Make sure you have time to devote to your puppy's care.

understand a particular breed's needs, you'll avoid getting a dog that's going to need time that you don't have to give. Also, if a dog that needs a lot of exercise is not given ample space, he can turn morose and destructive.

You also will have to take time to train the dog, take him to the veterinarian, and take him outside several times a day, not always at the most convenient times.

Cost

As mentioned earlier, getting a mixed-breed dog will cost you a lot less than a purebred dog from a breeder or a pet shop. However, wherever you get your dog, you will incur some immediate and continuing medical costs. For one thing, a new dog needs to be checked out by a vet and needs to get a variety of shots right away. There are facilities that will do much of this for free or for a discount, but at some point you will have to bear the burden of care yourself, and periodic visits to the vet for regular checkups and shots can add up. Over the

How Much Do Dog Owners Care?

Dogs add a tremendous amount of joy to peoples' lives, and owners care deeply about their dogs, something they demonstrate by their actions. Indeed, R. T. Nielson's random phone surveys revealed some astonishing things:

• Some dog owners report that a dog is more important to their lives than sex, spiritual life, friends, career, or car.

• 9 out of 10 dog owners give their dogs gifts at Christmas and on their birthdays.

• 30 percent of all dog owners carry a picture of their dog in their wallets; 80 percent report that they bought a food bowl—some custom made—for their dogs.

• 25 percent of the owners surveyed said they have missed work because of their dog's illnesses.

• 46 percent of owners who do not have a doggie door open their doors for their pets at least a dozen times a day.

And in other surveys, when asked why they owned dogs, companionship, love, and company were cited by 95 percent of owners, and 74 percent indicated that their dogs are considered another child in the family.

course of a dog's life, it will cost you thousands of dollars to care for him. Also, some costs are unexpected, such as an emergency visit to a vet.

Feeding your dog also costs money, and the larger the dog, the more food you'll need. There will also be a need to pay for equipment, such as leashes, collars, crates, and toys. Dogs love their toys, and there are a variety of safe bones and toys, like Nylabones®, from which to choose.

Grooming

Some dogs require more grooming than others. For example, longhaired dogs, such as spaniels and setters, require a lot more brushing than shorthaired breeds such as the Boxer and Greyhound. But a breed like the Poodle, with clipped hair and shaved portions on his body, is a grooming career in itself.

If you don't want to get involved in grooming, you can, of course, farm the chore out to a professional. Today, there are places where you can take your dog or that will come to you in a mobile van that contains the supplies and equipment needed to do a complete grooming.

Be wary, however. In addition to the cost of a professional groomer, which can be considerable, there is the possibility that you may not like the results. I remember once taking my little Benji look-alike, "Misty," to a dog grooming place, and when I returned to pick her up a few hours later, the shop had turned my hair-awry little dog into a clipped and combed little dandy that I hardly recognized. The groomer, of course, was beaming with pride.

Dog ownership is a big responsibility.

Some breeds need more grooming than others.

Each dog has his own individual personality.

Trainability

When selecting a breed, one should realize that some breeds are easier to train and housetrain than others. Some dogs are more eager to please, some are more bullheaded, and some have a personality that gets easily distracted and has trouble focusing on the trainer's commands. Such dogs include Irish Setters, German Shorthaired Pointers, Black and Tan Coonhounds, and some Boxers, Pulis, Fox Terriers, Doberman Pinschers, Vizlas, and Norwegian Elkhounds.

On the other hand, some dogs may be so smart that they question everything and want to do things their way. The result is the same as if they were slow–they're harder to train. Unless socialized, which means exposed to other dogs and experiences, and trained early, these dogs can be a nightmare, constantly pacing, chewing anything within reach, barking and whining when left alone, jumping up on strangers–even when leashed–and becoming very territorial.

Age

The cliché says, "You can't teach an old dog new tricks," but it's not really true. You can teach an old dog new things; it just may be not as easy. The older dog can be set in his ways; he's not the malleable material the puppy was. But old dogs can be taught basic things like heel, come, and stay, commands that will make for a much better companion. Do not let the fact that the dog is mature dissuade you from taking him home.

An adult dog may be the right addition to your household.

Consider getting a puppy after he's completely weaned from his mother and used to frolicking around on his own. Pups that are 8 to 12 weeks old usually work out quite well. Of course, most puppies will be weaned from their moms by six weeks of age, but the extra time with her is important because it lets them interact with their littermates, engaging in puppy fights and other behavior that gradually shapes their own particular personalities.

On the other hand, you don't want to get a puppy that has had no socialization in his early life, say three months of age or older, because bonding is key in raising a happy pet. After this age, bonding becomes difficult. Also, by this time, the dog may have developed undesirable traits.

One client of a dog trainer friend of mine brought his new Schnauzer in, complaining that the dog was very difficult to relate to, and that he seemed to "guard" his territory scrupulously. The trainer told the client that the reason the dog had these traits was because he was too old when he had gotten him, and that the dog came from a pet shop, where he resided in a wire cage without relating to any other living creatures. Territorialism was bound to develop, and aggressive guarding of his territory is an offshoot of this problem.

Bonding is the key to raising a happy puppy.

Dog Years and Human Years

The idea that one year in a dog's life equals seven years of human life is not exactly true. (Indeed, some dogs live to 20 years or more, which would mean 140 plus!) There are a greater number of dog years associated with a young dog than an older dog. For example, a dog of 6 years of age will have aged about 45 years; at 10 years of age, he's like a person who's 65; at 12 years of age, a person of 75; and at 15 years of age, a person of 90.

Fascinating Facts

The world's oldest dog, according to the Guinness Book of Pet Records, is an Australian Cattle dog named "Bluey" from Victoria, Australia. He died when he was almost 29 years old—146 human years.

Part 1

If you are just getting a dog for companionship, an older dog can be ideal, particularly if you don't have the physical ability or time to train a puppy.

Life Span

Whenever one of our pets had reached the end of her days, I was always unanimously elected by my kids and wife to take her to the vet to have her euthanized. It was a task that, no matter how many times I did it, I never got used to. I particularly remember taking Misty for what turned out to be her final visit. The vet examined her and concurred with my amateur assessment: Misty's time on this earth was over.

I started to cry when I placed her on the floor to show the vet how she could not walk, and when I kissed her good-bye and the vet took her from my arms, I really started to sob,

The following is a listing of dogs and how long, in general, you can expect them to live.

√ 7-10 years — Cavalier King Charles Spaniel, Great Dane, Newfoundland

√ 9-11 years — French Bulldog, Bloodhound, Boxer, Chow Chow, St. Bernard

√ 10-13 years — Airedale Terrier, Dalmatian, German Shepherd, Scottish Terrier

√ 12-16 years — Beagle, Bichon Frise, Collie, Doberman, Papillon, Pomeranian

√ 14-16 years — Boston Terrier, Cairn Terrier, Cocker Spaniel, Welsh Corgi, Golden Retriever, Irish Setter, Jack Russell Terrier, Maltese, Standard Poodle, Miniature Schnauzer, Shih Tzu, West Highland White Terrier, Yorkshire Terrier

√ 15-18 years — Chihuahua, Dachshund, Miniature and Toy Poodles

because it was not only Misty's life that was ending. It was symbolic of what someday would happen to all of us. And there was something else–we wouldn't have Misty or the sheer joy she brought to our lives anymore.

I do not want to be morbid, but a dog's life span may be a factor for you when considering which breed to select. In a sense, the longer the dog lives, the longer you put off the inevitable moment. To put that another way, you can love a dog that only lives 8 years just as much as you can love one that lives 20 years. You can put off that painful moment until later rather than sooner with certain breeds; yet, length of life may not matter to you at all.

What is the life span of various dogs? In general, vets will tell you that the larger the dog, the shorter his life span, even when the dog gets good, regular medical care. For example, a St. Bernard can begin to slow down at just 4 years of age and have a life expectancy of just 7 to 11 years. On the other hand, a Chihuahua, the smallest breed of dog, can live 18 years or more. In general, mixed breeds live longer than purebred dogs, and mixed breeds whose genes are predominantly those of the smaller breeds will live longer. Also, certain breeds can carry genetic diseases that will impact their life expectancies. More information on these conditions is discussed later in the book.

Make sure the puppy you choose is bright eyed and healthy looking.

How to Spot a Healthy Dog

√ Check the eyes. They should be clear, and there should be no evidence of discharge.

√ Check the ears. The inside of the ears should also be clear, not red or swollen. They should have no offensive odor and should not be sensitive when touched.

√ Check the mouth. Pull back the lips of the puppy and take a look at the teeth. They should be even and white, and the gums should be healthy looking. The breath should not have a foul odor.

√ Check the dog's coat. It should be healthy looking and have no bare spots. Run your hand through the coat from the tail end of the dog to the front and look for tiny black specks on the skin, which may be the fecal deposits of fleas.

√ Check the skin. The skin itself should be firm, nonscaly, and free of any redness.

Health Check

Unless you are lucky enough to know a veterinarian who will accompany you while you search for a pet, you should do a basic health check on any dog you plan to buy. If you are buying a purebred dog, it's a good idea to contact one of the breed clubs and get some tips from members on what to check for in the breed before you buy. Make sure that you ask the breeder if she has experienced any health problems in her line. If she claims to know nothing about any health problems in the breed, go elsewhere.

Before you buy a dog, you should make an arrangement with the seller for a "grace period" —a few days—during which you are allowed to return the dog. It's during this time that you can get the dog fully

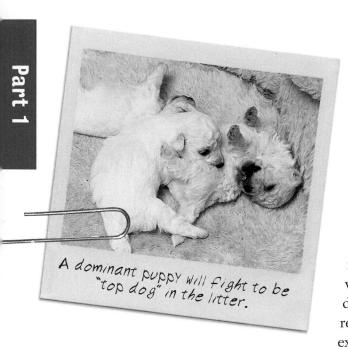

A dominant puppy will fight to be "top dog" in the litter.

examined by a vet to make sure he does not have any serious medical problems.

Temperament Tests

Before you choose a puppy, there are some amateur psychological tests that you can administer to determine its personality. The puppy should be alert, responsive, and questioning. To determine if the puppy possesses these qualities, gently toss a ball toward him. If he doesn't scurry after it like the proverbial mad dog but instead shies away, this might indicate that he has some behavioral problems that can become worse as he gets older. I remember one friend who told me that when his dog was a puppy, he never wanted to fetch sticks or scurry after a thrown ball. When the dog grew up, he manifested extreme fearfulness, unfortunately resulting in aggression, which my friend had to seek out expensive professional help to deal with.

There are some simple tests to evaluate the disposition of a puppy. Tell the breeder what you'd like to do, and if she balks, go to a different breeder.

First, you should observe the litter to see which dogs are most dominant, least dominant, or somewhere in between. An even-tempered puppy will not be a bully but will not back down when another puppy challenges him.

This puppy shows his submissive side—and gets a belly rub!

Another test to try is to clap your hands. A normal puppy will wonder where the sound is coming from; an overly fearful animal will take off and hide.

Next, roll the puppy on his back, which is a position of vulnerability, and stroke his belly. If he accepts the stroking, then he accepts you as the boss, which you must be in your relationship. If he doesn't accept the

What Can You Handle?

As you learn about the different traits inherent in the various types of dogs, be honest with yourself about who you are and what your personality can and cannot tolerate, as well as the feelings of other people in the house. For example, if patience is not one of your virtues, then certain dogs may not be for you. Years ago, for example, when the remake of the movie *101 Dalmatians* came out, the breed's popularity soared. However, people who obtained the dog later learned that Dalmatians are strong-willed and difficult to train, and many of these dogs ended up in animal shelters or were simply abandoned. Real-life endings were far less happy than in the movie. On the other hand, if the adopters had strong personalities, they might have looked on the strong-willed persona of the dog as a challenge and even liked the dog for his willfulness. Of course, what you will have to handle may not be so obvious with dogs of mixed parentage, but if you try to determine what breed is dominant in the dog, you should be okay.

stroking without fighting, it means he has a high dominance or alpha level and may have difficulty accepting you as the leader of the pack, making him difficult to work with. Conversely, if the puppy goes limp and seemed terrified, he will be controlled by fear, which, again, can be a difficult situation.

Despite the testing, you may still want that overly submissive or overly dominant dog. Your best bet is to get professional help right away when training him. A professional trainer can make the dog a desirable pet, but it will take a lot of time and expense.

Do Your Homework

Research is crucial when you have to make a decision, and it also applies to choosing a dog. Dogs come in many different "flavors." Like humans, they are essentially the same, but we all have different needs, wants, and personalities. The idea is to make your needs, wants, and personality fit the dog's like a hand would fit a glove.

Choose a breed that will fit in with your family and lifestyle.

Research the breeds you're interested in thoroughly

Can't Change Mother Nature

While training can help you to better control your dog, it is not going to change his basic instincts. "Why would anyone want to?" says trainer Linda Rudolph. "That's part of an individual dog's charm."

Some of the other characteristics to determine about the dog include how active the breed is, and whether he barks a lot, roams, digs, runs after things, loves water, herds, etc.

until you have a good grasp of what will work best for you, your family members, and your lifestyle. In order to do this, it's important to define your particular goals first. What do you want the dog for? Guard dog, companion, bird dog? Will the dog be living with children?

To get a better idea of whether the dog will fit or not, imagine that he has the personality and habits of a person who's coming to live with you. Would it bother you if the person were high strung, aggressive, or wanted to go out all the time? Dogs can want all those things–and more.

Also know that dogs of the same breed can differ drastically, and it's best to keep this in mind, no matter what you learn about a breed. In other words, the information given here is a general guide that can alert you to what to look for and expect, but it is only general. You buy a very specific, particular animal, and it's this dog that you want to find out about. The following are all excellent resources for discovering information that will help determine what breed fits best with you.

Breeders

Breeders are of particular importance because, despite our reverence for the

A Presidential Problem

In his book, *Dog Training by Bash*, trainer Bashkim Dibra pointed out the importance of getting the right dog by telling the story of a dog owned by President Reagan and his wife Nancy.

The dog, a Bouvier des Flandres, a large, stubborn, herding dog, required close attention and training, neither of which the Reagans were able to provide. Gradually, the dog became a problem, jumping up on Nancy, playfully nipping at the President's heels until she drew blood, and following her herding instinct by herding President Reagan.

The situation reached the meltdown stage when it was reported in the media, and the Reagans realized that they had to get a different dog. Word got out, and soon they were the proud recipients of a male Cavalier King Charles Spaniel. The dog had a temperament and style perfectly suited to White House living, and he turned out to be an ideal pet, ultimately becoming so popular with kids that the Reagans would send out pictures of him signed with a paw print.

Meanwhile, the other dog, nicknamed "Lucky," was shipped to their ranch in Santa Barbara, California, where she did quite well.

written word (particularly our own), talking with folks who have owned and bred particular breeds and have experiences with them can be invaluable–the best information you can get. You can and should ask questions until you are solidly convinced that a particular breed is for you.

When you go to a professional breeder, be aware that the information given to you may be a little biased, colored by the love the person has for the breed. Breeding and caring for this particular dog may be "their life," as someone once said, and you may get a highly positive but distorted picture, just as you would if you were talking to proud parents about their children.

The information you get is likely to be of a higher quality if you obtain it from a breeder who goes into an impassioned monologue that asserts all kinds of reasons why people *shouldn't* own the breed he or she is gaga about. Indeed, a friend of mine said that a breeder once told him that because he had young kids, the last thing in the world he should do was get a Doberman Pinscher. "Meanwhile," my friend said, "we did get one, and it was great–and then got another."

Chalk it up to overprotectiveness–breeders only want the best for their dogs. If you find a breeder like that, and you can convince her that you're the right owner for one of her dogs, you can be sure that you are getting the best-quality puppy.

You also have to find a breeder who is a true breeder and not a "backyard breeder"–someone who just raises the breed to make a quick buck. You want someone who is devoted to the breed and is constantly striving to improve it. One good way to do this is to search the Internet and locate and contact breed clubs for specific breeds or go to the American Kennel Club website, which lists the names and numbers of legitimate breeders. Before you buy from any breeder, check her out thoroughly. Get

Healthy puppies are a reflection of their breeder's good care.

references and when you talk with her, pay attention to your gut feeling.

Another way to find a good breeder is to attend dog shows. The benched shows are best, because breeders have to show their dogs on benches and are available to talk before or after they show their dogs. Today, there are benched shows in Detroit, San Francisco, Philadelphia, Chicago, and the World Series of dog shows, the Westminster Kennel Club held in New York City in February. Find the breed you want, then sit down and talk with the breeder when she's not showing her dog.

You may be in for a surprise. "One thing I often find in good breeders," says a dog-trainer friend of mine, "is that they will often interrogate the buyer. They don't want the dog going into the hands of a person who's not right for the dog."

One good question to ask a breeder is where the puppies live as they grow up. If she says in her kennel, think twice. Love and socializing are keys to raising a good dog. The best place to raise a dog is in the house with the rest of his pack.

Dog shows are a great place to learn about different breeds.

Veterinarians

Veterinarians can furnish invaluable information about a dog's possible medical problems, as well as temperament, simply because he or she sees so many dogs. I remember discussing an American Staffordshire Terrier with one vet and he told me, "They have tremendously strong jaws." From that moment on, I was able to understand why they were such superb fighters.

Trainers

There is a hilarious short story called "Black Angels" written by Bruce Jay Friedman that concerns a man hiring a bunch of floor sanders to redo his floors. They do such a fabulous job–resanding it a dozen times, applying a dozen coats of finish (At one point, the foreman tells the homeowner, "It'll start to shape up once we get the 22nd coat on it.")–and all at such a low price that the man, who is having some marital problems, asks the foreman of this fabulous crew if he'd like to act as his psychiatrist.

The man committed a common sin. He assumed that because the refinishers were so knowledgeable and skilled at doing floors, they could apply the same skills to any subject.

So it is with trainers. Just because someone is an expert on Doberman Pinschers, it doesn't mean that he will be an expert on Boston Terriers. Not all trainers train all dogs–you should seek out someone to talk to who has specific know-how with your particular breed of dog.

Friends and Neighbors

If a friend owns the type of dog you're interested in, pick his or her brain. People like nothing better than to volunteer their expertise on things, including dogs. I remember years ago, for example, when I didn't know a Maltese from a malted, I was walking down the block when a young lady was in the process of retrieving this incredibly cute, tiny dog with long white hair.

I asked, "What kind of dog is that?"

"A Maltese," she said.

"How is it as a pet?"

The first thing she enthused about was that despite the length of his hair, he "didn't shed" and then went into a laundry list of superlatives about the dog. Over the years, I learned that the superlatives were deserved, and my neighbor's information was accurate.

Books

If you buy any books on breeds, be aware that just because something is written, it doesn't make it true. Like the breeders who extol the virtues of their breeds, writers may be loath to

Ask your friends about their dog's personality.

Hero Dogs

The dog's devotion to man is legendary, and history is dotted with instances of how dogs have served mankind, even when their own lives were in danger. Undoubtedly, one of the most famous was from Switzerland and was called the "Barry Dog," named after a St. Bernard that is said to have helped save the lives of 40 people trapped in blizzards. There is a statue of Barry that can be seen in the Natural History Museum in Bern.

mention any negative traits the dog has. If they don't discuss negatives or if they issue a lot of euphemisms rather than using plain language, be wary. Learn to read between the lines. No living creature is perfect—and this includes the dog.

The Internet

There is a tremendous amount of information available on the Internet, but you should be aware that there is no way to guarantee its accuracy. As one trainer said, "It's overrun with self-styled experts."

On the other hand, the AKC and ASPCA have sites, and so do universities, such as Cornell, which has a veterinary school, and the information found there will be impeccable.

Where to Get Your Dog
Breeders

There are a variety of places from which to obtain a dog, and to some degree, it depends on what kind of dog you want. If you want a purebred dog, then the most desirable place to go is to a dedicated breeder.

At a breeder, you'll be able to see the puppy's mom and dad, as well as his brothers and sisters. Take a look at them and observe them interacting with each other. Do they seem like good offspring or are they shy or overly aggressive? On top of your observations, the breeder will be able to give you instant personality profiles, as well.

The breeder will also know—and you should ask—about what kind of vaccinations, deworming, and other health care the puppy has received. She can also tell you whether or not the puppy is housetrained, obedience trained, and what kind of food he has been fed and on what schedule.

If you buy a purebred from a breeder, you can expect to carry away some paperwork. Indeed, if you don't get any, start asking yourself questions about the legitimacy of the breeder.

One important piece of paperwork is the sales contract. This lays out your responsibilities, as well as the breeder's, including health and temperament guarantees and your right to return the dog. The contract is usually very simple, unless you intend to show the dog, which can make it more complex.

You should also get the puppy's health records. This will show the kind of medical care the dog has received and if the breed is subject to a particular genetic problem, along with any testing that has been done on his parents. Your pup's parents' health clearances should also be included.

Your puppy's parents should be healthy and well adjusted.

The breeder should provide you with a pedigree, which is the genealogy of your dog that goes back three generations and indicates if your pup's relatives did well in various competitions.

A registration certificate or application should also be included in the paperwork. This will be necessary to register the dog at the AKC. You should also be given detailed instructions on how to care for the dog, including the brand of food that he has been given and a feeding schedule to follow.

The Pound

In general, today's dog pounds are a far cry from the places they once were. The dogs are well cared for, and you can be sure that the dogs housed there are in very good shape. Shelter workers also will be able to tell you a lot about a dog's personality, because they interact with each animal on a daily basis. If the dog has an obvious bad habit, it can be hard, expensive, or even impossible to cure him of it if he's mature—and you shouldn't think you can.

Shelters are excellent places to find canine companions.

The best advice is to get a dog that seems problem free, or if he does have problems, make sure that they are problems that you can live with.

To emphasize the point about medical problems: No one can be absolutely sure that any dog they get will not be incubating one or more diseases, no matter how great the dog looks. This is why it's important, when you buy a dog, to isolate it for a week or so from any other pets and see if disease develops. Also, as suggested, take him to a vet immediately so that the vet can check the dog out for things such as worms (from examining fecal material) or the dangerous contagious diseases like parvovirus, leptospirosis, coronavirus, or canine hepatitis.

Rescue Groups

These are folks in breed clubs who care for unwanted dogs of their breed. For example, one club in my area cares for Greyhounds that have outlived their usefulness to track owners and would otherwise be killed. Rescue groups have both grown dogs and puppies, and their members are just the kind of breeder you should be looking for.

Key Points

• The dog you select must fit your personality, your family, and your lifestyle. The key to finding the right dog is research.

• Smaller dogs live longer than large ones.

• Unless the dog is going to be shown, neutering is mandatory.

• Different breeds have different characteristics, such as herding and retrieving, and training is not going to change these traits; it just helps to control them.

• Individual dogs in the same breed can differ greatly, so it's important to evaluate one-on-one before selecting a puppy.

• Evaluation of any dog should include both health and temperament tests.

• The Internet, books, and magazines are important for information, but the most important way to gather facts is by talking with people who own the particular breed or are familiar with the dog's background and parentage. Asking questions can be tremendously helpful when making a decision.

• Some breeders will exaggerate a dog's good points and downplay the bad, while other breeders will accent the bad points and not the good because they don't feel anyone can take care of the breed as well as they can.

• The great advantage of getting a purebred dog is that the breeder can usually predict what good habits and what bad habits the dog will have: You know what you're buying. The advantage of a mixed-breed dog is that he will usually have fewer health problems than a purebred dog.

• Some breeders are better than others. Take great care who you buy your dog from. Your best bet is to select a breeder from one registered at the AKC.

• Get the dog examined by a vet before committing to keep him.

• Getting a dog is a long commitment, perhaps 15 to 20 years. Make sure you are ready for the responsibility.

A Guide to the Breeds

Just the other day, I was in a bakery getting my morning bagel and coffee when an older woman came in with one black and one gray Whippet, a breed, in case you're not familiar with it, that looks like a smaller version of a Greyhound.

"How do you like them?" I asked.

"Love 'em," she replied.

"Any problems?"

"Well the gray one, who's two years younger than the other one, is aggressive toward other dogs."

Each breed has its own personality.

"Did you try to get it worked out of him?"

"Oh yes," the woman said, "we tried everything."

The incident illustrates a profound truth about dog breeds.

While a particular breed will share general characteristics, not all dogs are exactly alike.

Top 40 AKC Registered Dogs

1. Labrador Retriever	21. Bulldog
2. Golden Retriever	22. Basset Hound
3. German Shepherd	23. Doberman Pinscher
4. Dachshund	24. German Shorthaired Pointer
5. Beagle	25. Bichon Frise
6. Poodle	26. English Springer Spaniel
7. Yorkshire Terrier	27. Pembroke Welsh Corgi
8. Chihuahua	28. Great Dane
9. Boxer	29. Pekingese
10. Shih Tzu	30. West Highland White Terrier
11. Rottweiler	31. Brittany
12. Pomeranian	32. Weimaraner
13. Miniature Schnauzer	33. Lhasa Apso
14. Cocker Spaniel	34. Collie
15. Pug	35. Australian Shepherd
16. Shetland Sheepdog	36. Saint Bernard
17. Miniature Pinscher	37. Chinese Shar Pei
18. Boston Terrier	38. Akita
19. Siberian Husky	39. Mastiff
20. Maltese	40. Cairn Terrier

In Year 2000

When you consider a breed, remember that dogs have individual characteristics. They are individuals; some may be aggressive, some moderately behaved, some submissive, some nervous, and so on. Like people, they have specific characteristics, which is why your research must not only be broad, but also focused on individuality.

Currently, the AKC recognizes 150 breeds, and some are far more popular than others. The AKC, which maintains a purebred registry or list of dogs, describes a purebred dog as follows: "The sire and the dam of a dog are members of a recognized breed and that the ancestry of a dog consists of the same breed over many generations." It should be understood that being on the AKC list does not mean that the dog has good health and temperament. The AKC does not evaluate dogs in this way. It just means that the breed has satisfied AKC breed-purity criteria for registration.

American Kennel Club

The American Kennel Club (AKC) is the most prestigious dog group in the country. It was founded on September 17, 1884 by a group of amateur sportsmen for the purpose of promoting the health and welfare of purebred dogs, as well as interest in them. It also maintains a registry of purebred dogs. People register their dogs, which are allowed into the AKC as long as they physically adhere to the standards of the organization. For example, the official standard for a Greyhound, in brief, would be a head that is long and narrow; a neck that is long and muscular without throatiness; shoulders that are muscular without being loaded; perfectly straight forelegs; a deep chest; a muscular and broad back; loins that have good muscle, are well arched, and well cut up the flanks; hindquarters that are long and muscular; feet that are hard and close, more like the feet of a rabbit than a cat; a tail long and fine that tapers and curves upward slightly; a coat that is short, smooth, and firm; and a weight that is 65 to 70 pounds for males and 60 to 65 pounds for bitches. All Greyhounds should be bred to the ideal of the standard, and when dogs are competing in conformation competition, they are judged against the standard of the breed.

The AKC also administers a variety of training courses and contests that are conducted by hundreds of local club members throughout the country. It also has an investigative arm that ensures that the groups comprising its membership maintain the standards of the entire group. All of this helps to ensure the integrity of the dogs registered.

You can contact the AKC by using the following information:

American Kennel Club

260 Madison Avenue	5580 Centerview Drive	919-233-3600
New York, New York 10016	*or* Raleigh, North Carolina 27606	919-233-9767
		www.akc.org

The following is a guide to the top 40 breeds, in terms of AKC registrations, as well as a random selection of other popular breeds. It includes descriptions, traits, and levels of trainability, as well as activity levels, which one trainer, Captain Arthur Haggerty, considers the most important trait of all. The information given is what is generally true.

Purebred Dogs

Breeds tend to go in and out of popularity, depending on a variety of factors, but perhaps mainly because of the media–TV, movies, newspapers, and magazines. If a breed gets "good press," then it becomes popular. If not, its popularity declines. The number of dogs that are registered by the AKC is an important measure of this popularity.

A classic example of the media influencing dog ownership occurred years ago regarding the German Shepherd. It was the star of the *Rin Tin Tin* and *Strongheart* movies, and registrations at the AKC soared to 1500 a month. However, most new owners did not research what the dog was really like, and neither did the media (who, truth be known, usually puts sensationalism above anything else). When the media started reporting stories about the Shepherd being involved in attacks on people, the registration dropped to well

Top Ten

As of the year 2000, the top ten dogs in order of registrations are:

1) Labrador Retriever: 172,841 registrations, up 12 percent from 1999 and 2 times as many as the second most popular breed

2) Golden Retriever: 66,300 registrations, up 6 percent

3) German Shepherd: 57, 660 registrations, up 1 percent

4) Dachshund: 54, 026 registrations, up 6 percent

5) Beagle: 52, 026 registrations, up 8 percent

6) Poodle: 45,868 registrations, up 1 percent

7) Yorkshire Terrier: 43, 868 registrations, up 7 percent

8) Chihuahua: 43, 096 registrations, up 17 percent

9) Boxer: 38,803 registrations, up 11 percent

10) Shih Tzu: 37,599 registrations, up 9 percent

under 100 a month. Now, as responsible breeding practices are being used, the German Shepherd has returned to popularity.

The AKC puts purebred dogs into seven different categories or groups, mainly based on what they were bred to do. The groups are Sporting, Non-Sporting, Herding, Hound, Working, Terrier, and Toy.

The Sporting Group

Sporting dogs have been bred to hunt birds. The group includes spaniels, pointers, setters, and retrievers, as well as a group of unclassified "others." Some sporting dogs are bred to flush birds from their cover; others are bred to point—to let their tails extend straight back and hold their heads rigid—to the location of the birds. Others retrieve the game for the hunter after it is shot.

Sporting dogs vary in size from 9 to 80 pounds and have great stamina. They are friendly, active, and don't bark a lot—although some bay—and they like children. As you might expect, most of them need space to run, but a number of them are good dogs for apartment life if they are regularly exercised.

Irish Setter

The Irish Setter would be hard to beat in a beauty contest. At one time he was black and white, but these colors were bred out so that today his coat is moderately long, and his color varies from a golden-red-chestnut to mahogany. He weighs about 60 pounds and stands around 26 inches at the shoulders or withers.

The setter, or red setter, has been in America since just after the Civil War, but he was running around the British Isles for 200 years as a hunting dog, and apparently a superb

> Though still in the top 15, the Rottweiler dropped 11 percent in popularity, perhaps because of the media coverage. (One survey declared the Rottweiler to be the most dangerous dog of the decade.) The Rottweiler is a dog that needs strong, consistent training, which some owners don't provide, mainly because they don't know they're supposed to.

> It should be noted that it is not really possible to train fundamental characteristics out of a breed. What you can do is control the dog to the point where the training overrides the impulses. For example, if you were walking a setter, and a bird suddenly appeared, hundreds and perhaps thousands of years of genetic conditioning would be telling that dog to go after the bird. Your training will keep him by your side, but the instinct to run will be still be there.

Dogs in the Sporting Group

Small- to Medium-Sized Breeds (24 to 50 pounds):	
American Water Spaniel	English Setter
Brittany	Flat-Coated Retriever
Cocker Spaniel	German Shorthaired Pointer
English Cocker Spaniel	German Wirehaired Pointer
English Springer Spaniel	Golden Retriever
Sussex Spaniel	Gordon Setter
Welsh Springer Spaniel	Irish Setter
Large Breeds (50 to 80 pounds):	Irish Water Spaniel
Chesapeake Bay Retriever	Labrador Retriever
Clumber Spaniel	Pointer
Curly-Coated Retriever	Vizsla
	Weimaraner
	Wirehaired Pointing Griffon

Irish Setter

one. Breeders in America noted how beautiful he was, brought him across "the pond," and started to breed him mainly for beauty, going for the reddish hues and breeding out black and white. Today, no black- and-white coloration is allowed by the AKC in any dog regarded as a true Irish Setter.

The Irish Setter is very active, stubborn, and may be hard to housetrain (as I discovered personally). He is a lovable, mild-mannered dog but is commonly characterized with a variety of euphemisms that add up to this: He's not that bright and matures slowly, and is therefore difficult to train overall. He needs an owner that is willing to devote a lot of time and effort to training.

English Setter

As one bird hunter said after seeing his English Setter point a pheasant (head and tail pointed in a line) when the bird flew up from cover: "For that one ten-second experience and the memory of the picture, it would be worth keeping the dog in my kennel for a whole year."

English Setters are extremely beautiful dogs with a personality to match. Their coats are long and flat, colored either tan, blue, lemon, orange, liver, or black and white. They stand about 25 inches and weigh up to around 70 pounds.

The English Setter is descended from particular beautiful hunting dogs of Spain that go back at least 400 years. There are different types; the "field-trial" type developed by the American hunters is a very fast dog.

English Setters require a lot of space and exercise, but they also make wonderful house pets. They are very affectionate and have a great capacity for receiving affection themselves. They are also relatively inactive indoors, but are difficult to housetrain.

English Setter

German Shorthaired Pointer

The German Shorthaired Pointer is an example of how great breeders can produce a great dog. Breeding a variety of dogs with a sort of multipurpose goal in mind, breeders were successful in coming up with a dog that is good at retrieving on land and water, trailing, pointing, and scenting, all mixed with great endurance. The breed is also very smart, loving, and loyal. Many people who have never seen a duck lift off a lake have one of these dogs as a pet.

The German Shorthaired Pointer—so named because his coat is very short (though he does shed)—does have some problems, but not insurmountable ones. He can be difficult to housetrain and obedience train. In either case, starting early with a firm approach will help.

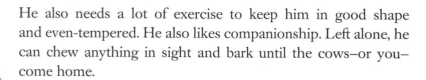

Spaniels

Spaniels are bred to run ahead of hunters and flush hidden birds into flight so that the hunter can have a shot at them. Because the hunter is not supposed to shoot long distances, the spaniel runs close by, and, when the bird falls, stands ready until the hunter gives a command. Then the spaniel retrieves the bird for him. In general, these dogs are outgoing, active, friendly, and obedient.

He also needs a lot of exercise to keep him in good shape and even-tempered. He also likes companionship. Left alone, he can chew anything in sight and bark until the cows—or you—come home.

Even when exercised regularly, he's still a very active dog indoors. He is fine for older children, but younger kids might find him too big and excitable to handle. He is medium sized, standing 23 to 25 inches and weighing in at 35 to 70 pounds.

Gordon Setter

The Gordon Setter is usually one of three dogs cited by many people as the best dog in the world in terms of intelligence and reliability. He lives for his family, and it would be impossible to find a dog that gets more attached to his people. On top of these qualities, he is a beautiful dog that has a longish black coat with tan feathering. The Gordon Setter is a mid-sized dog, weighing 55 to 80 pounds and standing 24 to 27 inches.

On the negative side, the Gordon is stubborn and can be hard to housetrain. Like other setters, once he acquires a bad habit, it is very difficult to break him of it. He also may retain a strong desire to roam.

Cocker Spaniel

In 1975, a Cocker Spaniel named Ida Hurst Belle won Best in Show at the Westminster Kennel Club, and the popularity of the dog went through the roof: Following her victory, one of every four dogs registered at the AKC was a Cocker Spaniel.

Popularity brought about greed, and overbreeding damaged the dog's temperament. As veterinarian Leon V. Whitney pointed out, "There was clique of breeders who arranged it so that only Cockers with huge, wooly,

Cocker Spaniel

clipped coats had a chance of winning." The popularity of the breed plummeted because few people wanted such a dog, and even fewer wanted a dog with a bad temperament.

Fortunately, due to responsible and dedicated breeders, the Cocker is back on track. Their popularity has now returned; today, the Cocker Spaniel is number 14 on the AKC registration list.

Housetraining Cocker Spaniels can be difficult, though they have all the wonderful personality traits of spaniels in general. They need exercise and are active indoors.

Cocker Spaniels (the name "Cocker" is said to derived from the dog's hunting woodcock) stand 14 to 15 inches high and weigh 23 to 28 pounds. They come in various hues, including black with white markings. Their long, silky hair needs regular brushing and trimming by an expert.

Welsh Springer Spaniel

The Springer Spaniels

There are two versions of the Springer–the English Springer Spaniel and the Welsh Springer Spaniel. The English Springer is bigger, standing 8 to 20 inches high and weighing up to 55 pounds. The Welsh is smaller at 16 or 17 inches and weighing no more than 40 pounds. Their coats also differ. The English Springer has a coat of medium length and may be flat and wavy, while the Welsh has a flat coat that is thick and silky. The Springer Spaniel's coat must be regularly brushed out, or it can become quite messy.

English Springer Spaniel

Brittany

Their colors vary, too. The English may have black, liver, blue, white, tan, and a wide variety of color combinations, while their Welsh cousin's coat is a rich, dark, red-and-white color.

If you want an all-purpose dog, it would be hard to do better than either Springer Spaniel. Says one owner about his Welsh Springer, "This dog is fantastic. In addition to being a great bird dog–it can retrieve game from the water with the best–it has also served me well as a hound, is great around my four kids, and makes a great watchdog. Have I left out anything?"

Brittany

The best place for a Brittany is in the water, retrieving a bird; the dog is marvelously suited to this type of work. He is also a pointer. Brittanys are not big. They are about 20 inches tall and weigh up to 40 pounds. Their coats are liver and white or orange and white and are flat, wavy, and a little coarse, rather than curly or silky like other spaniels.

One problem with this dog is that he tends to be aggressive with strangers and can bite. For best results, it is important to start socializing a Brittany early.

Clumber Spaniel

This is a very easygoing, gentle dog. He is the largest of the spaniels, is excellent with kids, and has no problems with strange dogs. He averages 16 to 19 inches and weighs 35 to 65 pounds. He has a short, slightly wavy coat that is white with lemon markings.

He does have a couple of habits to consider: He snores, sneezes, and drools. Exercise is good for this dog, not only because he is a hunting dog, but because he tends to overeat and is not that active indoors.

Irish Water Spaniel

This breed began in Ireland as a water retriever. The Irish Water Spaniel stands around 23 inches tall and weighs between 55 and 65 pounds. He has a liver-colored, dense, short, curly coat that sheds very little; however, his coat should be trimmed once a week.

The Irish Water Spaniel can be protective, stubborn, and timid, and tends to be a one-person dog, though as long as he is well socialized, he should not have any problems with other family members, children, or strange dogs.

Chesapeake Bay Retriever

The origins of this breed in America can actually be traced to a shipwreck. In 1807, an English ship went down in heavy seas off the coast of Maryland. Luckily, an American ship named the *Canton* was close by, and the crew, as well as several dogs on board, was saved. Two Newfoundland puppies were given to the Americans in thanks for saving their lives.

Retrievers

As the name suggests, the job of retrievers is to retrieve game that has been felled by the hunter, without doing any damage to the bird with their teeth or mouth.

These two dogs mated and later mixed with American retriever-like dogs. By the late 1900s, hunters had produced what is today known as the Chesapeake Bay Retriever.

Chesapeakes, which weigh around 75 pounds and stand 26 inches, can be of any solid color from dark to light brown and may have a white spot on their chests. Their coats, built for enduring cold, are wooly at the base but short at the top. As such, they can swim in frigid water.

The retrievers are bred to retrieve game and return it to the hunter.

Chesapeake Bay Retriever

Golden Retriever

Labrador Retriever

They make excellent pets, are great with kids, and are very good watchdogs. However, they are retrievers, of course, and like wide-open spaces and plenty of exercise.

Golden Retriever

If some dogs are in public relations hell, this dog is in public relations heaven. The classic Golden Retriever is one of the finest family dogs you can get, an affectionate loving creature that is kind to everyone.

However, in recent years, greed has become a factor in the breed, and these dogs have been overbred to the point that an owner has to be very careful when getting one. Today, some of them have been so poorly bred that they range from being submissive to aggressive, something previously unheard of in this breed. Again, it is very important to find a dedicated breeder and make sure you get a true example of the breed.

The Golden Retriever is an active dog that must be trained, and he is highly trainable. He loves to please his master. The best obedience dogs are almost always Goldens.

The Golden Retriever is a big dog, standing 21 to 24 inches at the withers and weighing 55 to 75 pounds. He is a beautiful dog, with a coat that ranges in color from dark red to pale cream. Dogs with the darkest red usually have the strongest field instincts.

Although they are a delight to live with, there are some health concerns with Golden Retrievers, including bloat, cancer, and hip dysplasia. Golden Retrievers also need plenty of exercise.

Labrador Retriever

During World War II, the United States military thought it would be a good idea to train the Labrador Retriever, a big powerful dog, to be an attack dog. There was only one problem–the dog's instincts wouldn't allow it, and he failed to make the grade because he lacked aggression. It is a small wonder that this dog is at the top of the AKC's registration list.

The Labrador stands up to 24 to 25 inches high and weighs in at 55 to 70 pounds. He has a short, shiny coat that may be black, chocolate, or yellow, and he does shed a bit. Because he is a retriever, it is no small wonder that he loves the water.

Labradors should be exercised and allowed to run regularly. They will be active indoors, but are sweet and gentle with children and have such great personalities that they are often used as guide dogs for the blind and assistance dogs for the physically challenged. Although wonderful creatures, they are intelligent and can be single-minded, so they need early training.

Weimaraner

The Weimaraner is a dog that requires early socialization. He also requires a lot of area to run and exercise, but he is generally easy to care for. He is a large dog, standing around 27 inches high and weighing approximately 85 pounds. He has a beautiful, short, gray coat and a docked tail.

Weimaraner

The Weimaraner is assertive and will dominate if allowed. He is very active indoors and will need a lot of training to avoid becoming destructive. He also is a runner, and if he isn't allowed to do it outdoors, he may engage in a one-dog steeplechase race through the rooms of your home. He also may be difficult to housetrain. Because of his high energy level and assertive nature, he is not really a great dog for kids, but has no problem co-existing with other dogs.

Part 1

Bull Terrier

The Terrier Group

A dog trainer once said, "You live with terriers, you do not own them." Originally bred to hunt vermin such as rats, terriers have very tenacious, stubborn natures. It's important to train them well so that they don't become aggressive and challenge your authority.

They come in two versions–the short-legged terrier and the long-legged terrier. The short-legged terrier was trained to go into dens and burrows for small game, while the long-legged terrier was trained to dig for game. Terriers are aggressive and courageous, have lots of stamina, and are very good watchdogs. They normally don't like other animals but are loyal to their masters. Their natures make it incumbent on owners to socialize them early in their lives.

Dogs in the Terrier Group

Small- to Medium-Sized Breeds (15 to 50 pounds):	
Australian Terrier	Miniature Bull Terrier
Bedlington Terrier	Miniature Schnauzer
Border Terrier	Norfolk Terrier
Bull Terrier	Norwich Terrier
Cairn Terrier	Scottish Terrier
Dandie Dinmont Terrier	Sealyham Terrier
Smooth Fox Terrier	Skye Terrier
Wire Fox Terrier	Soft Coated Wheaten Terrier
Irish Terrier	Staffordshire Bull Terrier
Kerry Blue Terrier	Welsh Terrier
Lakeland Terrier	West Highland White Terrier
Manchester Terrier (Standard)	**Large Breeds (50 to 80 pounds):**
	Airedale Terrier
	American Staffordshire Terrier

Bull Terrier

This odd-looking dog with a cone-shaped head came into prominence when he was paraded around the battlefields of Europe by General George "Blood 'n Guts" Patton, the American general who played a significant role in World War II. The Bull Terrier was an extension of Patton's aggressive personality, and the dog is every inch a battler. He was once trained for pit fighting and is quite powerful, although he is not particularly large. He stands an average of 18 inches high, weighs 35 to 55 pounds, and has a short coat that may be white or colored, the latter brindle or fawn, with white chest, feet, and blaze.

> ## Hand Stripping
> Some terriers have distinctive double coats, consisting of soft undercoats and wiry jackets that need special grooming. Many are plucked or stripped by hand, which is a time-consuming process that gives them an unmistakable appearance.

The secret to controlling this dog, as with so many others, is early and consistent training.

Dandie Dinmont Terrier

This dog makes a wonderful pet, but is probably better suited for adults than for children. The Dandie Dinmont is not stubborn, but he knows what he likes. He may be hard to housetrain, is fairly active indoors, and needs a fair amount of exercise. He learns very quickly and is considered one of the smartest terriers. Medically, the breed may develop kidney problems, back problems, or ear mites.

The Dandie Dinmont is 8 to 11 inches tall and weighs between 18 and 24 pounds. His long, rough coat, which is pepper or mustard colored, must be groomed professionally twice a week, which can get expensive.

Wire Fox Terrier

Fox Terriers

My sister and I owned one of these dogs when I was seven years old, and I remember him with fondness. There are two types of Fox Terriers—the Smooth Fox Terrier and the Wire Fox Terrier. The difference is the coat; one has a smooth coat, the other a wire-haired coat, both white with markings. The breed is lively indoors and on the small size, usually not more than 15 inches tall and 16 to 18 pounds.

This dog is naturally stubborn and bold. He may pick fights with other dogs and may bark more than other breeds.

West Highland White Terrier

This small dog, which is 10 inches high and weighs 15 to 20 pounds, originated in the mid-19th century in Scotland. Like many terriers, he was originally developed for hunting vermin.

West Highland Terriers come in darker colors, but the white-coated dog was particularly prized because his distinctive coat made it easy for hunters to spot him, and the chances of his being accidentally shot—which sometimes occurred with his dark-coated brethren—was minimal.

West Highland White Terrier

Happily, unlike some other terriers, Westies are easy to train and housetrain. They are very active indoors and out, but because they're small, they're easy to keep as house pets. They like people and are not aggressive.

One might think that it would be difficult to keep the Westie's coat white, but it can be maintained with brushing and the regular use of a dry shampoo.

American Staffordshire Terrier

The Am Staf is a sweet dog when with his own family, but it is a very powerful breed, standing 17 to 19 inches tall and weighing up to 70 pounds. He is a guard dog and watchdog by nature and can be very protective when his family is not around—it would be difficult for a

American Staffordshire Terrier

child to walk an Am Staf by herself. A very active dog, he can be hard to housetrain. His coat is short and easy to groom, and he may be any color, but most (about 80 percent) are liver and white or black and tan.

Miniature Schnauzer

This gray, wire-haired dog has energy to spare. His ears, cropped when he's a puppy, along with his beard, give him a very distinctive appearance. The Schnauzer comes in various sizes (Giant, Standard, and Miniature), but the Miniature Schnauzer is 12 to 14 inches high and weighs less than 15 pounds. He is an active dog that tends to bark. As terriers go, he is easily controlled with training.

Cairn Terrier

You may recognize the Cairn Terrier–he was the little dog that accompanied Dorothy in the movie *The Wizard of Oz*. His original job was to hunt rodents and foxes, and he will bark when a stranger comes to the door. This affectionate little dog stands 9 to 10 inches high, weighs 13 to 14 pounds, and is a highly adaptable breed. The Cairn Terrier can live in apartments and is easy to housetrain; but when training, it should be remembered that he is a terrier and can be aggressive and stubborn.

Australian Terrier

This terrier stands around 10 inches and weighs 12 to 14 pounds. He is a sturdy little dog with a shaggy blue and tan or sandy red coat, which

The Pit Bull

The Pit Bull has been much maligned in American society, and the fact is that he is more frequently involved in attacks on people than other types of dog. Pit Bulls have been bred for fighting, and although illegal, there are still many dog fights in the United States.

However, the Pit Bull's reputation has not been earned by the dog himself, but by the irresponsible breeders and owners that encourage the breed's aggressive tendencies. Despite their fearsome reputation, they have an equally wonderful reputation as pets when they are bred for good temperament, well socialized at an early age, and obedience trained.

Australian Terrier

requires about 15 minutes of grooming a week. He is a bit active indoors, needs outdoor exercise, and is a good dog with kids who are gentle and respectful.

Bedlington Terrier

When groomed for the show ring, the Bedlington Terrier looks like a lamb. He stands up to 16 inches high and weighs 17 to 23 pounds. He has a curly white coat that requires professional trimming, and caring for him can be very time consuming. He is somewhat active and barks more than other breeds, and he can be aggressive with other dogs.

Border Terrier

This is a terrier with a very even disposition. He likes everyone and is wonderful with children, but like most terriers, can be aggressive with other animals. A hardy dog, he stands from 13 to 15 inches tall and weighs 15 pounds. His short, rough coat may be red, grizzle-and-tan, blue-and-tan, or red, and needs to be trimmed twice a week.

The Hound Group

There are 19 breeds of hound recognized by the AKC. These dogs have been bred to hunt by either scent or sound and are classified that way. Either a sighthound or scenthound would make an excellent pet.

Their sizes vary according to the kinds of game they were designed to hunt. For example, the relatively small Dachshunds were classically hunters of badger, while huge Irish Wolfhounds, as the name suggests, were used to hunt wolves. As one might expect, these dogs have acutely developed senses of smell and sight. Early training is important in order to control these dogs because they can be chewers and howlers.

Whippets

Whippet

This dog seems to personify Coco Chanel's motto, "You can't be too beautiful or too thin." The Whippet, which may be black, tan, or gray, stands only 22 inches high and weighs around 28 pounds. If a dog can be described as gorgeous, then this is an apt description for the Whippet. He is slim and sleek, a kind of thinner,

Dogs in the Hound Group

Very Small Breeds (under 20 pounds):	American Foxhound
Dachshunds—Standard and Miniature	English Foxhound
Small- to Medium-Sized Breeds (20 to 50 pounds):	Greyhound
	Ibizan Hound
Basenji	Pharaoh Hound
Basset Hound	Rhodesian Ridgeback
Beagle	Saluki
Harrier	**Giant Breeds (more than 80 pounds):**
Norwegian Elkhound	Bloodhound
Petit Basset Griffon Vendeen	Borzoi
Whippet	Irish Wolfhound
Large Breeds (50 to 80 pounds):	Otterhound
Afghan Hound	Scottish Deerhound
Black and Tan Coonhound	

smaller version of a Greyhound, and brings to mind a fashion model parading down a runway.

In fact, Whippets are very much like Greyhounds. Sighthounds by nature, they can make difficult pets because they will run after anything, such as the neighbor's cat, paying no mind to the traffic streaming back and forth in the roadway.

Despite this tendency, many people keep Whippets as pets, perhaps because they are so beautiful. One should be wary, however, when bringing a Whippet into a house with very young kids. This fragile dog needs gentle handling and has little patience for someone pulling his tail.

Bloodhound

Most people, when they think of Bloodhounds, conjure up the image of a bunch of loudly baying dogs straining together on the ends of leashes held by a law enforcement agent going after a criminal. In fact, Bloodhounds are used for tracking lost persons because of their excellent sense of smell and are quite successful at their jobs.

Bloodhound

Basset Hound

However, there is another side to this breed. Bloodhounds are affectionate, even-tempered dogs, but they are not designed to be kept indoors, particularly in a small apartment. Outdoor dogs requiring plenty of exercise, they are happiest following their noses and excel at events like tracking.

Basset Hound

Because of his unique appearance, the Basset Hound became popular through exposure on television shows and in the media, but he also makes a fine pet. His silky ears and smooth coat make him pleasant to handle. The Basset has short legs, which were developed over the years so he could hunt in dense cover; however, he does not possess a lot of endurance. A Basset is a nose behind the Bloodhound in having the best scenting ability of all dogs. Interestingly, the Basset's long ears have a purpose in tracking: They sweep across the ground, stirring up scent that may otherwise have been lost.

Basset Hounds are great with kids because they don't get ruffled when mistreated; indeed, they are probably the most difficult of all dogs to agitate. Because they were developed for country living, Basset Hounds do best in wide-open spaces, but they are adaptable to apartment living. If they don't have a lot of room to run, they must be walked fairly frequently–three or four times a day–to give them the exercise they need.

There are two possible difficulties with Basset Hounds. First, since their ears are long, they tend to make a mess when eating, and they are known to distribute a lot of slobber around the house. Second, because of their easygoing, mellow attitudes, it takes a lot of patience and effort on the part of the owner to housetrain and obedience train them.

The Origins of the Hot Dog

The hot dog actually was started at the turn of the century by ballpark concessionaire Harry M. Stevens, who capitalized on the public's craving for hot but sloppy sausage dishes by serving it in a roll and adding a liberal swab of hot mustard. The snack was an immediate success, and vendors traipsed up and down the stairs at stadiums selling liberal amounts of them.

Then, a local New York cartoonist named Tad, created a drawing showing a Dachshund, which had a long, red body, dubbing it a "hot dog," after which the term slipped into the language.

Then, rumors started that hot dogs were in fact made with dog meat, and sales plummeted to the point where laws had to be enacted banning the use of the term. Today, of course, the vast majority of people do not interpret it that way, and hot dogs remain a favorite all over the country.

Dachshund

The "hot dog" is available, like frankfurters, in a variety of sizes, ranging from 5 to 20 pounds and is classified as either Miniature or Standard. He may be shorthaired, wirehaired, or longhaired. The Dachshund comes in a variety of hues, including red, brown with brownish spots, or black with tan spots.

The Dachshund comes from Germany, and his name means "badger dog," referring to his original purpose–to go to ground for badger and other game. He makes a great pet and because of his bark, he is something of a watchdog. He can be confined to an apartment without a problem; however, although his hunting skills have been more or less bred out, he does need regular exercise.

Dachshunds can suffer from possible back trouble, which is hereditary and genetic, so owners should be aware that it could occur and talk to the breeder about any problems in the line that they are considering.

Longhaired Dachshund

Greyhound

The Greyhound, which is the fastest canine alive, tends to run pell mell after anything that moves, including a cat across a busy street, so it can be a difficult breed to manage. In modern times, Greyhounds have been bred to run on a track after a mechanical rabbit, although they were originally bred to chase and dispatch coyotes, foxes, rabbits, and even wolves. They would work in packs, like wolves, and were extremely successful in catching their prey. Because of their instinct to run, they can be difficult dogs to own, though many people have adopted them from racetracks when their careers are over. Slim, slender, gentle, graceful-looking dogs, they weigh in at about 50 pounds.

Greyhounds are usually easy to train and housetrain, but they need lots of daily exercise. Their chasing instinct is so strong that it is recommended that one keeps them fenced in or on a leash when outside.

Afghan Hound

The image of the Afghan Hound is regal and aristocratic–this is a dog that one imagines at the end of an expensive leash being walked by the butler outside an English manor. The dog has a long history. Some people trace it back to ancient Egypt 5,000 to 6,000 years ago, and it is said that the Afghan was preferred by the kings of the time and used as a hunting and coursing animal. The Western world first became aware of the breed in the 19th century, when it was discovered in Afghanistan and surrounding areas and brought to England.

The Afghan Hound is particularly good on hilly terrain, has a great ability to jump, can stand great extremes of weather, and, like other hounds, can run for hours. He was used to hunt leopards, which surely indicates that he is more than just beautiful, but tough as well.

He is a large dog, weighing in at 60 to 65 pounds and standing around 28 inches tall at the withers. Despite his purportedly regal heritage, beauty, and dynamism, the Afghan Hound can make a good pet, but in fairness to the dog, the owner should be willing to exercise him for hours every day.

Because his hair is long and silky, it mats rather easily, and anyone who gets an Afghan Hound should be prepared to clip the hair and comb it out daily. The dog is relatively inactive indoors and can be a slow learner. Medically, the breed can fall victim to cataracts and hip dysplasia and should be bred with this in mind.

Irish Wolfhound

The Irish Wolfhound is one the largest, strongest breeds of dog. He stands almost a yard (33 inches) at the withers and weighs 140 pounds or more. He has a wiry coat that comes in a variety of colors–tan, black, red, gray, and brindle.

Part 1

Originally, he was bred in Ireland to hunt wolf and giant elk, which stood over six feet tall at the shoulder. At one point, because of severe exportation from Ireland, the breed almost became extinct, but then a Scotsman in the British army named Captain George A. Graham set about to restore the breed and succeeded.

The Irish Wolfhound is big—and he was known to be bad. His great strength is blended with a heritage that goes back to Roman days when he was imported from Ireland and used in gladiatorial contests; however, the dog is not a bully, nor is he aggressive. He is generally sweet-tempered and calm and will demonstrate his loyalty and power only when provoked. He is fairly inactive indoors, but should be given exercise regularly and room to be comfortable. An Irish Wolfhound is meant to spend a lot of time in an outdoor environment where he can run. A Wolfhound makes an excellent watchdog for which no training is required; his ability comes naturally, something that farmers know and appreciate. This dog is easy to housetrain and train.

Irish Wolfhound

One important note: You need to take care in the way that you handle the Irish Wolfhound. He is a very sensitive dog and can become depressed and shy if treated insensitively.

Beagle

Some dogs become popular, and then their popularity fades. However, some dogs remain in fashion all the time, and the Beagle is one of them. For example, the Beagle is currently ranked fifth on the AKC registration list, up eight percent from last year, and he has been in the top ten as long as one can remember.

Beagle

The Beagle is a small dog, standing around 15 inches at the withers and weighing between 15 and 30 pounds. He was originally bred in England and came to America in the latter part of the 19th century.

The Beagle, a scenthound, is bright, easygoing, and great with kids, but is also stubborn, bold, and can be difficult to housetrain. While bred to hunt–and able to issue a quite distinctive baying sound–there seems to be no problem keeping a Beagle in an apartment. However, make no mistake about it, he is a very active dog and needs lots of exercise.

Norwegian Elkhound

My mother and father owned Norwegian Elkhounds–and so did a lot of other people over the years. These dogs' bones have been found among those of Vikings dating 7,000 years ago.

This breed is generally regarded as one of the best ever developed. A Norwegian Elkhound looks something like a small German Shepherd, weighing about 50 pounds and standing 20 inches high, with gray fur with black tips. What I remember most about the one my mother and father owned was that his tail permanently curled upward in the back–I never saw it down.

The Norwegian Elkhound has the heart of a lion, which it has engaged in combat, and he has been used for all kinds of hunting, including bears and wolves. He has virtually unlimited stamina and is a superb watchdog. It is said that he is able to smell and hear things at distances up to three miles, which is astonishing. He has a distinct, high-pitched bark and barks more than other breeds. In addition to all of these wonderful qualities, the dog is gentle, playful, and very loyal.

Like most other hounds, Norwegian Elkhounds would not be happy as apartment dogs. They were bred to run and climb and would be a bit active indoors. They also shed heavily. This is a very smart breed, but if these dogs are not well trained, they may try to dominate their owners.

Borzoi

A Borzoi is quite impressive looking. He is a very large dog, standing 31 inches at the withers and weighing over 100 pounds. He is usually white, with a long, silky coat, and has an arched back and narrow snout.

It is said that the Borzoi was developed in Russia. A Duke imported Arabian Greyhounds as hunting dogs, but the first imports did not survive the brutal, bone-chilling Russian weather. The Duke is then said to have crossed them with a herding dog, which developed into the Wolfhound, and eventually developed into the Borzoi.

Borzois have tremendous speed and stamina. When hunting, they run in packs. They are another type of dog that seem ill-suited for apartment living, but if given regular exercise, this arrangement can work, because these dogs are calm and not that active.

Basenji

The most unusual characteristic of the Basenji is that he hardly every barks and makes few, if any, sounds, therefore he is known as the "barkless dog." The dog does make some noise– he actually sort of chortles or yodels when he's happy. Another unusual characteristic is that the Basenji cleans himself fastidiously like a cat, licking himself all over.

This breed originated in central Africa and was used for hunting. He is swift, powerful, and silent. Contrarily, his silence has put him in disfavor with American hunters. He is still used in Africa for hunting small game, including the vicious reed rat, a creature with long teeth weighing 12 to 20 pounds. In this endeavor, his silence is particularly valued.

Despite his great skills as a hunter, this little dog (16 to 17 inches tall and just 25 pounds) makes a wonderful pet, though he is very active indoors.

Basenji

The Working Group

The Working Group includes the wide variety of dogs developed to guard people and property, and all share some common characteristics. They are all large or very large and by nature can be aggressive and territorial with strangers. Many require a very firm hand and early discipline to control them. However, when they are bonded with people and socialized early, they can be very loyal and affectionate pets.

Dogs in the Working Group

Small- to Medium-Sized Breeds (20 to 50 pounds):	Alaskan Malamute
	Bernese Mountain Dog
Portuguese Water Dog	Bullmastiff
Standard Schnauzer	Great Dane
Large Breeds (50 to 80 pounds):	Great Pyrenees
Boxer	Greater Swiss Mountain Dog
Doberman Pinscher	Komondor
Giant Schnauzer	Kuvasz
Samoyed	Mastiff
Siberian Husky	Newfoundland
Giant Breeds (over 80 pounds):	Rottweiler
Akita	St. Bernard

Akita

Akita

The Akita originated in Japan, where it is an animal of mythic proportions. When someone is sick, he or she may be given a statue of an Akita to bring back good health. Statues of Akitas are also given to parents when a child is born.

The Akita is a loyal, noble, courageous dog that has long been used for hunting large, dangerous animals such as bear and wild boar. The breed was first brought to America by Helen Keller, who was given an Akita puppy as a gift by an American soldier in Japan after World War II. He may be any color including white, brindle, and pinto. He is a large dog, standing 24 to 28 inches, with a massive head, small ears, and a black tongue.

All of these assets and heritage notwithstanding, the Akita can be very difficult to handle. Again, overbreeding is the culprit. Akitas should be bred for good temperament above all else, and those that are not can be aggressive with other dogs, can be self-assured to the point of arrogance, and can try to dominate a household. More often than not, they also have some serious health concerns, including hair loss from a disease called sebaceous adenitis, or SA. Again, good breeding is the key to obtaining a good canine companion.

Mastiff

If you want a large dog, look no further than the Mastiff. The Mastiff stands up to 30 inches high and is muscular and heavy. He has long been renowned as a guard dog and fighting dog. Indeed, Caesar is said to have admired the way the breed fought by its British originators' side. There are many tall tales about Mastiffs fighting creatures such as elephants and lions, but they have even-tempered personalities and do not have trouble getting along with people.

Mastiff

St. Bernard

The St. Bernard achieved fame as the dog of choice at a refuge for people who traveled the treacherous, snowy paths through the Alps between Switzerland and Italy. It is estimated that they have been responsible for rescuing over 2,000 people.

One myth about St. Bernards is that they need a lot of exercise. In fact, they need only a little bit, as they spend most of their day snoozing. "When I first got my St. Bernard," my sister Jackie once said about her dog Brandy, "I thought he had sleeping sickness! He slept about 18 hours a day."

Saint Bernard

The St. Bernard comes in two sizes: large and very large, weighing over 100 pounds and standing 26 or 27 inches at the shoulders. This dog is generally a gentle giant, but one should take particular care with this breed to ensure that it does not suffer from aggression or orthopedic problems.

Great Dane

Despite his name, the Great Dane is a German breed of dog. At one time, the Great Dane was a hunting dog, but today he is mainly a showpiece, a beautiful moving statue with a good temperament that makes an excellent pet, assuming you can cope with his size: He stands 28 to 30 inches tall and weighs 120 to 150 pounds. Unhappily, he is likely the shortest-lived of all breeds; even with good care, he seldom lives longer than nine years.

The Great Dane comes in a variety of colors from fawn to black as well as harlequin, which is white with black spots. Curiously, the Great Dane has a relatively tiny bark for such a large dog, but he will use that bark incessantly in certain situations, such as when left alone at home.

Boxer

Boxer

The Boxer started his climb into the public consciousness perhaps 50 years ago, boomed in popularity, went into a decline, but has recently made a comeback. The current AKC figures show it in the ninth position in registration. Because of the breed's popularity, you should be particularly careful to get a dog with a calm disposition.

The Boxer is strictly a guard dog and is quite an impressive looking animal, with his muscular body, big chest, and close-cropped ears and tail. He is a large dog, standing 21 to 25 inches tall from the withers and weighing around 70 pounds. He has a short coat that comes in a variety of colors, including tan wearing "socks"–white paws that look like socks. Other variations of the breed may be white, dark brindle, and tan and white. He is a quick learner and rather active in the home; however, he makes a very manageable pet. Ideally, he would be ensconced in a place where he can run. One other negative aspect to owning a Boxer is that he snores and makes a snorting sound when sleeping, but this can be surgically corrected.

Doberman Pinscher

Around 1890, a man named Louis Doberman bred this part black-and-tan terrier, part Rottweiler, and part German Pinscher dog in Germany. The Doberman Pinscher stands up to 28 inches high and weighs in at around 75 pounds. He has a glossy coat that is black or tan and has yellow eyes–he makes quite an arresting package!

The breed has an image of being dangerous, and the fact is that he is not really the kind of dog that most people will find suitable. Indeed, the AKC official standard for the Doberman Pinscher says, "The judge shall dismiss from the ring any shy or vicious Doberman" and defines viciousness as a dog "that attempts to attack either the judge or its handler.... An aggressive or belligerent attitude toward other dogs shall not be deemed viciousness."

Doberman Pinscher

As a guard dog, however, the Doberman is excellent, and the breed has been depicted in this way in movies and on television. They have the tools to protect their territory, including the bark–a Doberman registers more barks per minute than any other dog. Incidentally, if you ever see a Doberman being used to track someone in the movies, you'll know that they aren't using the right kind of dog: the Doberman's ability to smell is limited, and he only would be able to detect fresh tracks.

Great Pyrenees

This dog, originating in the Pyrenees Mountains of France, is tall and strong, weighs 90 to 125 pounds, and is usually white or white with markings. The Great Pyrennes has been around a long, long time, perhaps 4,000 years, going back to the ancient Celts. He is good with kids as long as he is raised with them from puppyhood, but is

Great Pyrenees

reserved with strangers; however, he has no problems with strange dogs. If you have sheep that need herding, look no further–the Great Pyrenees makes an excellent guard dog of both livestock and family.

Great Pyrenees are subject hip dysplasia and have a strong yen to roam. They shed heavily twice a year, and like all large dogs, the Great Pyrenees has a short life span.

Siberian Husky

The adaptability of the Siberian Husky is nothing short of amazing. Bred to carry sleigh loads over stupendously long distances, he can nevertheless make an acceptable pet in an apartment.

This is a strong breed with striking eyes and a very happy disposition. Huskies are active, however, and must be regularly walked and exercised. Still, they seldom are completely relaxed, and like a number of other breeds, they do not like to be left alone. They are also difficult to housetrain and train, but it can be done, and the time and effort you put into it is worth it.

Siberian Husky

The Siberian Husky is a medium-sized dog that stands, 20 to 23 inches tall and weighs in at 35 to 60 pounds. He has an outer coat and an inner coat, and sheds throughout the year, particularly in the late spring and early fall. Like a cat, he constantly icks himself, which makes bathing him an infrequent necessity.

He is generally good with children, but younger kids will be bowled over by his energy and size.

Rottweiler

The first thing that strikes you about the Rottweiler is his size. He is not only tall (he stands 21 to 27 inches), but he is also beefy, weighing up to around 115 pounds. Captain Haggerty describes the dog's image in his book, *How to Get Your Pet Into Show Business*: "Massive, forceful, mighty, and enormous. Rough, tough, powerful, and aggressive. Damian, the quintessential guard dog. A killer. Vicious. Not the breed for a commercial unless used to illustrate an indestructible, heavy-duty tire that was purchased primarily by the individual truck owner rather than the fleet owner."

Rottweiler

In the last decade, he has garnered an unenviable reputation, cited as having been involved in more fatal dog attacks than any other breed. If you do have not a dominant personality, stay away from this dog. The Rottweiler has a lot of power, and some authorities think that he is the toughest dog of all.

There is no question that this is a big, aggressive dog, but when a dog has an aggression or a behavior problem, it's almost always the breeder or owner who have failed them, either by poor breeding or improper training. A well-bred and well-socialized Rottweiler can make a good pet, providing he has the proper training.

Alaskan Malamute

The Alaskan Malamute is one of a number of Arctic dogs originating with the Malamutes, a native tribe found in the northwest part of

Alaskan Malamute

Alaska that settled on the shores of Kotzebue Sound. The Malamute tribe was very impressive. Writers spoke of its members as being tall, skilled, and monogamous–a happy, hardworking people. Their dogs are just as impressive. They were used to pull sleds in their native land and are said to be affectionate, particularly with children, and loyal.

The Alaskan Malamute weighs between 75 and 85 pounds and stands 23 to 25 inches tall. He has a double coat of hair to protect him against Arctic winters, the outside coat being coarse and the inside coat soft and thick, making an excellent insulation. His coat may be black and white, cinnamon and white, or gray and white. He must be groomed twice a week, and he also sheds heavily in season.

The dog learns rather slowly and may be hard to housetrain. He can also be stubborn and tends to be aggressive toward other dogs, which can be difficult to cure. Very active indoors, he needs a lot of exercise. Medically, Malamutes are subject to hip dysplasia and dwarfism. Despite all the above, they are still very popular with apartment dwellers because of their dispositions.

Bernese Mountain Dog

The Bernese Mountain Dog, which originated in Switzerland, is an excellent family dog and is great with children. He weighs 77 to 105 pounds and stands 21 to 27 inches at the withers. His coat is short, soft, wavy, and lies flat. By nature, he is a carting dog trained to pull loads for farmers and a natural guard dog. This dog learns very quickly, but he should be socialized early to curb a tendency toward timidity.

If you want a dog that wants to be around you, this is the breed to choose. He loves being with his pack–you and your family.

The Toy Group

Dogs in the Toy Group were developed as companions to people, and they're very good at their jobs. They are all small, but this doesn't mean they're timid. On the contrary, many are aggressive and will become the alpha–or pack leader–in the house if you allow them. They usually have long life spans, and many of them make very good watchdogs. Most are a little nervous around strangers but are good with people they know, including children.

Dogs in the Toy Group

All breeds in this group are small, ranging from 2 pounds to 20 pounds:	
Affenpinscher	Manchester Terrier—Toy
Brussels Griffon	Miniature Pinscher
Chihuahua	Papillion
Chinese Crested	Pekingese
English Toy Spaniel	Pomeranian
Italian Greyhound	Poodle—Toy
Japanese Chin	Pug
Maltese	Shih Tzu
	Silky Terrier
	Yorkshire Terrier

Affenpinscher

The Affenpinscher originated in Germany. His name translates into "monkey-terrier," because his face resembles a monkey with bushy eyebrows, black-rimmed dark eyes, and a prominent chin featuring a mustache and tuft of hair. The hair itself is shaggy and wiry.

The Affenpinscher is one of the oldest dogs and is believed to have played a major mating role in the development of a number of rough-coated breeds, such as the Miniature Schnauzer and Brussels Griffon. The dog stands around 10 inches high and weighs 7 to 8 pounds. He comes in various colors, including red, black, black and tan, and wheaten, which is a pale yellow or fawn color. His tail and ears are usually docked. His coat needs to occasionally be trimmed and stripped, but doesn't shed a lot.

Medically, the dog is subject to slipped stifle and fractures and is also sensitive to cold. The Affenpinscher

Affenpinscher

is a highly active dog that barks more than most breeds and is hard to housetrain. He may be a bit too high strung for some children, but is very loyal toward his owners.

English Toy Spaniel

If you want a laid-back, affectionate dog in a small package, this dog may work very well for you. In the 16th century, the dog was a favorite of Mary, Queen of Scots, and it is said that her English Toy Spaniel even accompanied her to the scaffold when she was hung.

English Toy Spaniels

The English Toy Spaniel stands around 9 inches and weighs 9 to 12 pounds. Inside the house, he is relatively inactive; he doesn't require a lot of exercise. He is also very friendly and sweet, though he sometimes can be a little stubborn. Considerate children and the elderly find the breed to be wonderfully tolerant.

There are four varieties of English Toy Spaniel. While the breed's history gets a little murky, it appears that all varieties of the dog up to King Charles the Second were black and tan. There are three other variations developed after the black and tan: the Prince Charles, which has three colors–white, black and tan; the Ruby, which is chestnut red; and the Blenheim, which is chestnut red and white. The coat is soft, wavy, and on the long side; grooming is normally done twice a week.

The English Toy Spaniel is relatively inactive indoors. Potential medical maladies include eye lacerations, respiratory problems, and slipped stifle, all of which can be controlled with good breeding practices.

Yorkshire Terrier

This elegant little dog, with his long, silky hair that stretches to the floor, is often associated with the rich and famous. However, the breed started out as a dog for the common man, particularly weavers, and as stated in the American Kennel Club's *The Complete Dog Book*, "It was so closely linked (weavers) that many facetious comments were made regarding the fine texture of its extremely long, silky coat terming it the ultimate product of the looms."

The Yorkie is a cute and lovely dog, weighing in between 3 and 7 pounds. His coat is a blend of metallic steel blue color on the body and tan on head, legs, chest, and breeches, and grooming his beautiful, silky coat is best done by a professional.

While he is characterized as a toy, he is more than willing to show the spirit of his terrier strain and background. A Yorkie is bright, bold, and assertive, which can make training difficult. He is also barky and active indoors. It's important not to let this small dog with a big heart get control of the house, or he can start snapping. The breed can also be aggressive toward larger dogs—size doesn't matter to a Yorkie.

Pug

Sturdier and more stable than other Toy dogs, the Pug makes a very good pet. He stands around 13 inches tall and weighs 14 to 18 pounds, and he has a distinctive, not very handsome face that makes him look like he's related to the Bulldog. His short coat comes in gray, fawn, or black. The Pug learns quickly, and he is good with kids but unpredictable with other dogs.

On the negative side, one has to be very careful about the Pug's eyes. They are large and prominent and tend to develop ulcers. The Pug is also subject to respiratory problems, which cause him to wheeze and snore, and he is very sensitive to heat prostration.

Pug

Pomeranian

The Pomeranian is a big dog in a small package. It is said that the Pomeranian, which is a member of the Spitz group of dogs, is descended from the large sled dogs of Lapland and Iceland, but he has been bred down to his present toy size. His entrance onto the world dog scene can be traced to Queen Victoria, who fell in love with the dog when she visited Florence, Italy, and brought one home with her. The love between the Queen and her Pom continued. In 1901, as she lay dying, she asked for her Pomeranian "Turi" to be brought to her, and the dog was lying beside her when she passed away.

Pomeranian

He stands about seven inches tall and weighs between three and seven pounds, though five pounds is about average. His coat comes in a wide variety of colors, including brown, beaver, chocolate, orange, blue, white, cream, and wolf-sable.

The Pomeranian, which primarily gets his name from his origins in Pomerania, is a dog with some personality conflicts. While he is fiercely loyal to his owner, he tends to be skittish or aggressive with outsiders, and definitely does not take well to kids.

Shih Tzu

The Shih Tzu is a rising star on the dog scene. Allowed on the registration list in 1969, it is the tenth most frequently registered dog at the American Kennel Club today.

Shih Tzu

The origins of the this little dog, which stands about 7 inches high, is 10 inches long, and weighs 15 pounds, is said by some people to have originated in the 17th century, where he was raised in Chinese regal circles by eunuchs who were competing for the good will of the emperors. The dog originally emigrated from the Byzantine Empire, whose leaders gave them to Chinese kings as a tribute. Before this, Buddhists say that the dog, whose name means "the lion" in Chinese (albeit a small lion), resulted from a mating of their deity and a lion.

The popularity of this little dog is understandable. He is adorable, with a face described as looking like a chrysanthemum, because his hair grows around his face. His coat, which comes in a wide variety of colors, is long and dense and sometimes wavy.

The Shih Tzu is a bit active indoors and can be hard to housetrain, but needs little exercise.

Chihuahua

These tiny dogs–they stand around five inches high and weigh all of six pounds–are normally very loyal to their owners. They're not that good around kids or strangers, but they do relate well to other Chihuahuas. The Chihuahua, incidentally, is one of the longest-lived breeds, some living to be 20 years of age. Their coats are smooth and tight, and they need very little grooming. Chihuahuas come in a variety of colors and need minimal exercise. They are, however, active and highly intelligent. They tend to be nervous and can bite; however, early socialization and training will help them greatly.

Pekingese

This dog of Chinese origin has been bred with a tremendous amount of courage, and he is often willing to take on other dogs of any size. Fortunately, most dogs will not fight such a miniature adversary; the "Peke" only stands about 8 to 9 inches high and weighs about 14 pounds.

Pekingese

While he makes an excellent house pet, his eyes need special care and concern. They are very large and bulbous and have no bone to protect them, which makes the dog susceptible to eye lacerations. Also, the hair on his face actually rubs against the eye and must be clipped or there is a risk of damage to the cornea. His coat, which is long and shaggy, needs regular attention.

Maltese

Around 1500 BC, when Malta was the cultural center of the world, the Maltese was its star. It is said that the queen's dogs ate off of dishes made from rare metals, including gold, and that the food itself was of the finest delicacies available at the time. If you lived during the reign of England's Queen Elizabeth I, you could expect to pay a small fortune for a Maltese, which translates to a rather large fortune today! Many who own this dog would say that he is worth the price–and more.

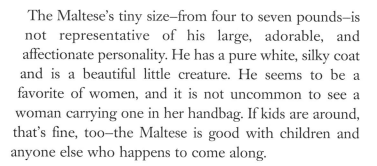

Maltese

The Maltese's tiny size—from four to seven pounds—is not representative of his large, adorable, and affectionate personality. He has a pure white, silky coat and is a beautiful little creature. He seems to be a favorite of women, and it is not uncommon to see a woman carrying one in her handbag. If kids are around, that's fine, too—the Maltese is good with children and anyone else who happens to come along.

The Maltese is very active indoors, and while generally friendly, he may snap at someone who is not careful with him. He may not be easy to housetrain, may become a picky eater, and can have dental, skin, and respiratory problems.

Brussels Griffon

Like the Affenpinscher, the Brussels Griffon had great "ratting" abilities around the farm, and his owners likely felt that if the Griffon, which was developed in Belgium, was crossed with the Affenpinscher, his abilities would be enhanced. Eventually, he was also crossed with the Pug, which has a smooth coat. This led to the development of smooth-coated, as well as rough, wiry-coated, Griffons. The latter type is far and away the more popular of the two. Grooming the smooth-haired kind is, of course, simpler than grooming the rough coat, which usually is done twice a week. His weight ranges from 10 to 12 pounds, and his coat colors may be red, black, black and tan, or beige.

Brussels Griffon

The Brussels Griffon wheezes, snores, and may overeat or be very picky about what he will ingest. Some dogs may experience medical problems such as slipped stifle, respiratory problems, and eye ailments. He is a quick learner, is very active indoors, and barks more than most breeds.

Italian Greyhound

The Italian Greyhound may look like a delicate, fragile dog, but he's not. As Toy dogs go, the Italian Greyhound is much less demanding than other breeds. The breed goes back at least 2,000 years, and those who have owned it form a *Who's Who* of royalty: James I of England, Frederick the Great of Prussia, Catherine the Great of Russia, Anne of Denmark, and Queen Victoria have all owned Italian Greyhounds. The dog is also much in evidence in the Renaissance paintings of Membling, Van der Weyden, Carpaccio, Giotto, Gerad David, and Hieronymus Bosch.

Experts agree that aside from his beauty, the most stunning thing about this dog is his affectionate disposition. He has no ego problems at all. He can fit into a family with children, although he tends to be high-strung and timid. He also has a very short, smooth coat and may be susceptible to chills, which is why you may often see him wearing a little jacket. The breed is a Greyhound in miniature, and it can weigh as little as 5 pounds, but as much as 15, though the average weight is 8 to 9 pounds. He learns quickly, although he may be hard to housetrain.

Italian Greyhounds

The Non-Sporting Group

The Non-Sporting dogs elude being categorized, except to say that the group consists of a potpourri of types, most developed simply to be companions to people. Many of the breeds were bred to work, but their jobs simply do not exist anymore. For example, the Dalmatian was bred to run alongside horse-drawn carriages, and since they outlawed bullbaiting, the Bulldog has become man's best friend instead of a fierce fighter.

Dalmatians are members of the Non-Sporting Group.

Part 1

Dogs in the Non-Sporting Group

Very Small Breeds (under 15 pounds):	French Bulldog
Schipperke	Keeshond
Tibetan Spaniel	Lhasa Apso
Small- to Medium-Sized Breeds (15 to 50 pounds):	Poodle—Miniature
	Shiba Inu
American Eskimo Dog	Tibetan Terrier
Bichon Frise	**Large Breeds (50 to 80 pounds):**
Boston Terrier	Chow Chow
Bulldog	Dalmatian
Shar Pei	Poodle—Standard
Finnish Spitz	

Lhasa Apso

Chinese Shar Pei

The Shar Pei has been around in China since at least 200 BC. Their name means "rough sandy coat." Very unusual looking dogs, their coats make them look like they have been sleeping in loose-fitting clothing for a long time. They are medium-sized, standing 18 to 20 inches tall and weighing up to 55 pounds, and very powerful. Because of their early popularity, overbreeding has resulted in an animal that can be aggressive. Moreover, they are beset with a variety of health problems, from skin disease to eye problems that require surgery while they're still puppies.

Lhasa Apso

The Lhasa Apso hails from Tibet and used to be prized as a guard of Tibetan royalty. His name is roughly translated into "Bark Lion Sentinel Dog." The dog became the center of attention and was therefore royally spoiled.

For eight centuries, the dog was prized in Tibet. Indeed, the Dalai Lama used to give one as a gift to important visitors, and quite a few were given to Chinese royalty. He is one of four dogs that came to America from Tibet.

The Lhasa Apso is a small dog, standing 11 inches high, and has either a white, black, gold, or brown thick coat that requires a lot of care.

Some people say that the Lhasa is not great with children, but others have had no difficulties. Many cite his aggressiveness and stubbornness: He may refuse to obey commands unless you are a dominant person. The dog does want a lot of attention, but if you are the type of person who can provide that attention, owning a Lhasa Apso should be a very good experience.

Schipperke

This is a Belgian dog that is very alert and energetic and makes a good watchdog as well as a pet.

Schipperkes are black and have a very strong constitution. Their tails are either bobbed or docked. They are small, standing 12 inches high and weighing around 18 pounds. One trainer, Brian Kilcommons, describes them as looking "sort of a cross between a fox and a miniature hyena." This dog is easy to train but can be very active indoors.

Schipperke

Boston Terrier

A friend of mine owned a very tiny Boston Terrier that was a bundle of nerves, with a bark like an oversized mouse. Another owner of one of these highly popular dogs warned: "Be wary about starting to play ball with your Boston. It will become a full-time job." Indeed, playing with toys, such as retrieving a ball, seems to be as important to this little dog as any other activity he can imagine.

His unique adorable looks make it hard to not to like the Boston Terrier. He is a true American dog, having been bred, as his name suggests, in Boston, by crossing the English

Boston Terrier

Bulldog with the White English Terrier. He stands around 17 inches high, weighs no more than 25 pounds, and his smooth, fine coat comes in brindle or black with white markings.

He can be a very high-strung dog, and may have a delicate digestive system. When he gets too excited, he can vomit, and he snores and snorts in his sleep. He also tends to be gassy, because he routinely gulps large quantities of air.

The Boston Terrier does not require a huge amount of space to gambol in, but he will appreciate a run every now and then, even though he can get used to apartment living. Early training is important with this dog. He also makes a very good watchdog, though he is not an excessive barker.

Bichon Frise

As a pet, it is hard to think of a dog that would be better than this little dynamo. For hundreds of years, going back to the Dark Ages, dogs have had one job–to entertain and love their masters. They do that superbly well.

Bichon Frise

Bichon Frises stand up to a foot high and weigh 11 to 20 pounds. Their coats are thick and wooly, but they do not shed much. On the other hand, a lot of brushing and trimming is required, and regular trips to a professional groomer are suggested to keep their coats from getting matted.

They are easy to train and housetrain, but one has to keep to a regular schedule to avoid accidents. They are very active indoors, but do not require a great deal of exercise.

Poodle

If you asked ten dog devotees what a Poodle looks like before being clipped, chances are that only a few would know. Well, just imagine what a large, mobile ball of steel wool looks like, and you have your answer.

The breed's image needs some work–they have an effete image (they are probably made fun of more than any other dog), because of the way their hair is clipped. (Poodles, incidentally, don't shed.) In fact, they are superb swimmers. Originally, they were clipped so that they could swim better–the Poodle's hair grows faster than any other dog breed.

Standard Poodle

Because of their swimming abilities, they were dubbed "pudelins," a German word that means "to splash in water," and the name was likely transmogrified into "Poodles." Poodles are one of the most intelligent dogs; indeed, many dog experts feel they are the most intelligent. They learn quickly and have a spry and happy personality.

There are three different poodle sizes: the Standard is over 15 inches high at the shoulder, the Miniature is between 10 and 15 inches, and the Toy is under 10 inches. Their weights range from 5 to 50 pounds.

Poodles may be black, white, blue, apricot, cream, or silver, and may even have spots. Some people may dye them pink, orange, blue–a practice that undoubtedly contributes to the dog's effeminate image.

Factors Affecting the Cost of a Breed

Some dogs will cost more than others for a variety of reasons:

√ If the dog has the potential to do well in dog shows or field trials (where his abilities are tested), he will cost extra.

√ If the breeder had to spend a lot on vet care as the dog was growing or on the mother and the delivery of the puppies, such as the Bulldog, which almost always needs to have a Caesarian section when giving birth, then those costs will be transferred to you.

√ If the litters are small or the breed is not popular and therefore not bred often or in high demand, the puppies will cost more.

Bulldog

Chow Chow

Bulldog

This breed, also called the English Bulldog, was first a symbol of English tenacity, and now has come to symbolize tenacity everywhere. If you say, "He's a real Bulldog," an explanation of someone's personality would not have to go any further.

The Bulldog is tenacious—one vet reported that he once saw a Bulldog bite into and snap off the leg of a larger dog during a fight.

As far as looks go, Bulldogs appear ugly to some people and gloriously gorgeous to others. (I remain noncommittal.) Suffice it to say that the dog has a pug nose, drooping jowls, and a wide, squat body with relatively short legs—there is no mistaking the Bulldog for another breed.

Bulldogs snore loudly, but this can be surgically corrected. Also, they are prone to heatstroke in the summer, so extra care should be exercised during this time to make sure that they are protected. They are not very active at all and are happiest hanging out with their families.

Chow Chow

The Chow Chow is distinguished from almost all other dogs by his black tongue and his furry, lion-like coat that comes in a variety of colors—red, cream, black, and blue. Chow Chow puppies are incredibly cute little balls of fur that people find hard to resist, but the breed has suffered from false advertising. Years ago, they were advertised as the dog that could do everything from guard the house to run down a fox, but this was not true. Chows, particularly male Chows, are unpredictable and may bite without warning. Because the full-grown dog weighs about 70 pounds, this is not something to be taken lightly. Indeed, one of the most laid-back trainers I know got a certain concerned look on his face when I asked him what he thought of the Chow.

Breeders have been aware of this tendency and have succeeded in breeding it out to some degree. In recent years, the dog's popularity has plummeted, which is a good thing, because the Chow has been overbred by unscrupulous breeders who are producing dogs that carry the worst characteristics. The best advice is to be very careful; research exactly what you're getting, and make absolutely sure you have a conscientious breeder before purchasing a dog.

Finnish Spitz

The Finnish Spitz, the national dog of Finland, almost became extinct. The history of the breed goes back thousands of years. The dog was originally bred by people migrating from Russia who settled in the far northern section of Finland, a land of 60,000 lakes. The dog's qualities were invaluable to hunters. He functioned by flushing out game, modulating his bark to direct the hunter to the quarry. Then, as time passed and a sort of cross-pollination occurred, the Finnish Spitz was gradually mated with other dogs, and the purity of the breed declined.

By 1880, they were almost gone; however, an original dog was spotted hunting in the northern forests of Finland. The hunters that found the dog were so impressed that they took the example of the best of the breed with them and started to breed them true again.

Eventually, the dog found his way into dog shows and to England, where he was nicknamed "Finkie." He later found his way to America in the late 1950s. In Finland, he is still used for hunting–and contests are held to measure his ability–but in America, he is more of a house pet, and one that is particularly fond of children.

The Finish Spitz comes in various shades of golden brown and stands from 15 to 20 inches tall.

French Bulldog

Originally, it seems that the ancestor of the French Bulldog was his often bellicose neighbor, the English Bulldog. But the breed's ancestors, which were Toy Bulldogs, did not find great acceptance in England, so they were shipped to France, where the breed as it is known today was developed.

French Bulldog

The modern French Bulldog has two distinguishing features: one is a head that is flat between the ears, while the other is an ear shape that resembles the pointed, triangular ear of a bat known as a "bat" ear. He weighs around 28 pounds and stands around a foot high.

In a sense, he has a curious personality. While he doesn't seem to have an affinity for kids, he does seem to like the elderly. He is very active indoors and needs outdoor exercise. He is essentially a sweet-tempered dog, and his short, smooth, glossy coat, which may be brindle, fawn, or white, is easy to keep clean.

French Bulldogs are prone to eye lacerations because of their protruding eyes and can suffer from respiratory problems.

Keeshond

The Keeshond has what one expert says is a strange smile—he looks menacing, although he has a very even-tempered personality. His smile notwithstanding, he has a definite fox-like look and a very fluffy blue or gray coat. He weighs from 35 to 40 pounds and stands 17 to 18 inches tall. He is excellent with kids and makes a good watchdog. He is a bit on the stubborn side, somewhat active indoors, and requires a lot of exercise.

The Herding Group

These dogs were developed to herd animals and to work in tandem with people. They are highly intelligent and often think independently. However, some of them may be overly sensitive and very shy if not bred properly. Early training and socialization will put them on the right path.

Bouvier des Flandres

The Bouvier des Flandres was almost wiped out in World War I. The area in which the dog lived was air raided, and many of the Bouviers that lived there were lost or died. Luckily, a number of owners were able to keep their dogs, and after the war, the breed started to develop into the outstanding dog it is today.

Dogs in the Herding Group

Small- to Medium-Sized Breeds (15 to 50 pounds):	Large Breeds (50 to 80 pounds):
Australian Cattle Dog	Australian Shepherd
Bearded Collie	Belgian Malinois
Border Collie	Belgian Sheepdog
Cardigan Welsh Corgi	Belgian Turvuren
Pembroke Welsh Corgi	Bouvier des Flandres
Puli	Briard
Shetland Sheepdog	Collie—Rough and Smooth
	German Shepherd
	Old English Sheepdog

The dog is essentially a cattle dog, developed by farmers and butchers who wanted a dog that would help them handle their cattle. Today's Bouvier is large, standing 22 to 27 inches tall and a weighing 80 to 110 pounds. His short coat, which may be black or gray, is good for rough weather; however, if you plan to show your dog, he should be trimmed and stripped with professional aplomb.

He is very smart, quick to learn, obedient, and alert, and makes an excellent watchdog, but he is also good with kids and very gentle. He likes a lot of exercise, but is relatively inactive when indoors.

One negative aspect of owning a Bouvier is that the breed is subject to bloat. Also, he is a very large dog that needs room to run–if you live in a cottage, think twice before purchasing a Bouvier des Flandres.

Briard

This dog, which originated in France, was bred as a herding dog, but also makes a good watchdog. The Briard is headstrong, and training must commence early to create a manageable dog, which will grow up to be between 70 and 90 pounds and stand between 22 and 27 inches high.

The Briard has a long, slightly wavy coat that may be just about any color but white. He must be groomed from one to two hours a week. He does shed, but hairs get trapped in his dense coat and must be rubbed out.

The Briard is a little slow to train. Though he is good with kids, he is reserved with strangers, and one never knows how he will interact with other dogs. This is a very active dog indoors or out, and he needs plenty of exercise.

Old English Sheepdogs

Old English Sheepdog

The Old English Sheepdog, which originated in England, is a big, shaggy, herding dog, standing at least 22 inches and weighing 75 to 90 pounds.

Anyone who gets one of these dogs should be prepared to spend time grooming him. The dog's long shaggy coat that must be brushed regularly. The coat may be black, steel blue, gray, blue merle, or blue gray in color.

As with so many dogs that have been very popular with the public, the Old English Sheepdog has been greedily bred by unscrupulous entrepreneurs. Unfortunately, the inherent qualities of the dog that one cherishes, such as being great with kids, may not be there. Indeed, a leading dog trainer once said it is the most unpredictable of all breeds. That is why it is particularly important that one obtains such a dog from a good breeder.

Puli

A Hungarian herding dog, someone once described the Puli as looking like a "mop with eyes." His black, gray, or white coat is very long and corded, like the strands of a mop, and it requires more than a little attention to keep it looking good. The Puli is a mid-sized dog, standing 19 inches high, and weighing an average of 30 pounds.

The Puli is a very quick learner and makes an excellent guard dog. This is a very active dog, and while he is high-spirited and protective, he is also willful and quick-tempered and not the dog for children, who may inadvertently anger him.

Note that some Pulik (the plural name of the dog) may be too high-strung for some people, and their barking can be bothersome. It is important to get this dog from a good breeder, not only to get an even-tempered pet, but also because Pulik are subject to hip dysplasia and skin ailments.

Shetland Sheepdog

The Shetland Sheepdog is indigenous to the Shetland Islands in Scotland. Like the Collie, which he resembles and is closely related to, he has a long, flowing coat and comes in the same colors. In fact, he is sometimes mistaken for a Collie, but is quite a bit smaller, standing only 13 to 16 inches high and weighing around 18 pounds.

Shetland Sheepdog

The Sheltie's beautiful coat must be regularly tended to, and he sheds for three weeks twice a year. He tends to bark more than other breeds and is very active, requiring a good deal of exercise. Although good with kids, he is not the kind of dog one can roughhouse with, because he can be a bit high-strung and timid. If one plans to own a Sheltie in the city, the dog should be introduced to that particular style of life sooner rather than later.

Medically speaking, the Sheltie is sometimes subject to epilepsy and Collie eye, which is a congenital defect of the optic nerve that impairs vision.

The Welsh Corgis

There are two types of Welsh Corgis—the Cardigan and the Pembroke. These dogs are very good at helping farmers and shepherds. They are active indoors and need a good amount of exercise.

Pembroke Welsh Corgi

Corgis may be sable, red, brindle, black, or merle with white markings. They have very short legs, stand about a foot high, and weigh 25 to 38 pounds.

German Shepherd

German Shepherds are one of the most well-known dogs for a number of reasons. They have been featured in many films, have served as guide dogs for the blind, and have proven to be good watchdogs and police dogs: When you see a police officer with a dog, more often that not, it's a German Shepherd.

This is one of the most intelligent dogs there is, and many would claim the best of all. However, overbreeding has resulted in a preponderance of shy, neurotic, aggressive dogs that actually outnumber the well-bred dogs. Take great care to find a responsible breeder before you get this formidable animal.

German Shepherds are a blend of beauty and power. They stand about 25 inches at the shoulder, and males weigh up to 85 pounds, while bitches may be normal weight at 60 pounds. Their coats may be black, gray, orange, or tan in color.

A German Shepherd is naturally assertive, so it's important to train and socialize him early. Also, it's important to have a vet thoroughly check out the dog before buying one: German Shepherds are prone to get hip dysplasia and a laundry list of other maladies.

Collie

There is probably not a dog with a better reputation than a Collie. Years on the "Lassie" television show established the breed forever as a gentle but brave dog (I've even seen Lassie take on a mountain lion in one episode).

German Shepherd

The Collie (the original name came from the name "Coally," from the highlands of Scotland) is in fact a dog with great heart–you couldn't find a more loyal canine companion.

There are two varieties of Collie: rough coated and smooth coated. In this country, the rough-coated dog is more popular. The coat colors may be blue merle, white, tan, black sable, and white, or any combination. Their coats should be brushed frequently, not only to bring out their beauty, but to impede the development of parasites on the skin. They are big dogs, standing around 26 inches high and weighing 75 pounds.

Collie

Because they are such popular dogs, they have been overbred by some breeders trying for a longer snout. Indeed, someone once commented that their heads were so narrow, they allowed little room for housing a brain. This implies a lack of intelligence, which is not true.

Collies are excellent with children, though sometimes a little skittish around strangers. They need a lot of exercise, and they commonly nip at the heels of running kids, the way they would if they were herding sheep. They also can be very shy and sensitive to noise.

Australian Shepherd

The Australian Shepherd is a highly intelligent dog, but can be problematic for the average person. His intelligence can make him a dominant personality, and he is often a very independent thinker. He is very active around the house and needs plenty of exercise, considering that he is a herding dog and was bred to help farmers round up sheep and cattle.

Australian Shepherd

Australian Shepherds are highly intelligent and easy to train, but definitely need to keep busy to stay out of trouble. They are very loyal, and if you give them jobs to do, they will be your partners for life.

Key Points

• Dogs are classified by the AKC into seven different groups: the Sporting Group, the Non-Sporting Group, the Hound Group, the Herding Group, the Terrier Group, the Toy Group, and the Working Group.

• The Sporting Group consists of dogs that have the instinct to hunt game, usually birds. Included among this group are spaniels, pointers, setters, and retrievers.

• The Non-Sporting Group consists of a kind of potpourri of dogs, but most are bred to be companions to people.

• The Hound Group consists of dogs born to track animals either by scent or sight. There are scenthounds, that track by nose, and sighthounds that track by sight.

• The Herding Group consists of dogs that were used in various countries to drive and herd livestock.

• The Terrier Group consists of dogs that were originally bred to hunt vermin. There are two types of terriers: long-legged and short-legged.

• The Toy Group consists of small-sized dogs that were bred to be companions to people.

• The Working Group consists of dogs that were bred to work for man, which usually included protecting human beings and/or their property.

• The media often influences the popularity of particular breeds of dog.

• One of the most important traits of a breed is activity level, because it will dictate the dog's behavior as a house pet and how much exercise he will require.

• The AKC registers dogs, which means it keeps a list of purebred animals. Dogs are allowed to register if it is certified that they conform to the breed standards that the AKC has established, such as size and weight, and if they can establish that they are purebred, meaning that their parents and the generations before them were the same breed.

• Having knowledge of a breed's traits is good for general guidance; however, the most important thing to consider when selecting a dog is an evaluation of the individual animal.

• No matter how intensely you train your dog, you won't be able to banish his fundamental traits, nor would you want to.

• Just because a dog is registered with the AKC doesn't mean he's healthy or has a good temperament. It just means he fulfills AKC breed standards. However, a breeder that adheres to AKC standard is dedicated to breeding a healthy, stable dog.

Understanding Your Dog

Understanding the dog's psychology and how they respond emotionally is an important element in successful training. Dogs need the same kind of emotional support and understanding that people require, especially when they're young. If they don't get this support, they can forever remain unattainable and unhappy, and perhaps grow up to be bad tempered and unpredictable. A trainer I know once said, "Wouldn't you?"

You can sum up what a dog needs in one word: love. As the saying goes, "Love is what makes the world go 'round"–and dogs are part of that world.
The first thing to understand is the crucial importance of a dog's puppyhood or childhood.

Your puppy will look to you for love and guidance.

Part 1

Puppies need love and affection from the very beginning.

Why Dogs Bark

Many people interpret a dog barking as a hostile act, that the dog is upset and is ready to attack. In fact, many times barking serves as the equivalent of an alarm bell, telling other members of the pack that there is an intruder. The intruder is then evaluated, and a determination is made as to whether it is friend of foe. If foe, an attack may ensue, but this is an entirely separate activity.

This is a period, generally the first four months of her life, when she is like a blank tablet, and is susceptible to the installation of all kinds of positive–or negative–behaviors. Time and time again, when we look for an explanation as to why a person or a dog does bad things, the answers are found in childhood or puppyhood. For example, when someone doesn't do well as an adult, we often hear some variation of, "Well, you know, he was mistreated as a child."

The cliché, "You can't teach an old dog new tricks" is not true. You can teach some things to an older dog, but her habits will already be established, and it will take considerable time and patience. The best time to teach the dog new tricks, however, is when the dog is young.

All You Need Is Love

The love that puppies show to their mothers, and later to their owners, does not come naturally to a dog. "This (love) is taught by their mothers and handlers between the ages of 4 and 14 weeks," says animal behaviorist Jean Craighead George in her book, *How to Talk to Your Animals*, "the critical period when a dog becomes happily adjusted to people or remains forever shy and antisocial, like a wild thing. Pups raised without human contact flee with their tails low at the sight of people and are as elusive as wolves."

George and other animal behaviorists agree that in order to develop a loving dog, it's important that the puppy is affectionately and frequently handled by human beings from the very beginning. In a word–nurtured.

Socialization

It is also important that a dog be socialized, which animal behaviorists define as the exposure to as many new

Nature vs. Nurture

The importance of nurturing has been demonstrated many times, not only as it relates to dogs, but also to people. One dramatic example of this occurred in the New York Foundling Hospital around the turn of the century. The orphan babies at the hospital were given the best of medical and physical care, lived in pristinely sanitary conditions, and in spite of this, were not surviving, except for, mysteriously, two or three. These babies, unlike so many of the others, thrived.

The authorities at the time searched high and low for the reason, which was finally unearthed: a cleaning lady. It was learned that each night she would come in to the baby ward, pick up those two or three babies, and treat them as if they were her own, kissing them, hugging them, and cooing to them. She nurtured them. Once this was discovered, nurturing was established on a sort of institutional scale, and the death rates of infants dropped dramatically.

experiences as possible. Socialization ensures that your puppy will not be afraid of something, as long as the puppy is allowed to approach the frightening thing and is allowed to desensitize it. During her first year, starting at an age when your vet suggests and after she has had all her shots, your puppy should be taken to different places, such as shopping malls, parks, neighborhoods other than your own, dog shows—just about anywhere you can dream up that will be a different environment. The puppy should be allowed to meet people of all ages and races, people in uniforms, little kids, senior citizens, and anyone else you can think of that will treat your puppy with affection and teach her to accept people.

It's almost certain that even a normally developing puppy will be a little wary of these experiences. After all, she's a little creature facing a big, perhaps noisy, new experience. For example, how would you feel if you were

Socialization ensures that your puppy will get along with other dogs.

Living Quarters

Dogs may be kept in a variety of places, including an apartment, despite the belief by many people that this constitutes cruel and unusual punishment. It doesn't. Millions of dogs live wonderful lives in apartments. Many dogs don't need wide open spaces to do well, and owners who keep their dogs in an apartment are scrupulous about walking them in all kinds of weather, taking them to the vet, and making sure that they are well groomed at all times.

Of course, some owners, either because of a mistaken notion that they don't want to confine their dogs or just because they're too lazy to walk them, let their dogs run free around the neighborhood. This is the sure road to tragedy. Dogs on the loose are susceptible to more illnesses than dogs that are controlled, and can be injured by cars, and other animals, including dogs.

When owners let their dogs roam around town, the owners are subject to more problems as well. Many communities prohibit free-roaming dogs because of possible harm to property or strangers, and one's neighbors can get quickly annoyed with dogs that do their business on their finely manicured lawns. Court records are full of cases involving one irate neighbor suing another because of a free-roaming pooch.

To sum it all up, a trained, controlled dog is a happy dog.

Make your puppy comfortable in his new home.

taken to a pet store (a good socializing spot, by the way) and forced to meet other people that looked nothing like you?

Of course, some dogs will try to avoid being socialized out of fear. You should encourage socializing gently but don't give in if the dog backs down. It's better to give your puppy a firm, "No!" if she acts frightened. If you soothe or coddle her, then whatever it is she's afraid of will be affirmed as something to be afraid of. Indeed, the more stressful the situation, the firmer your "No!" should be.

If your puppy goes forward in any situation and shows friendliness or enthusiasm, remember to encourage her. Praise is not only important to people, it is all-important to puppies as well.

When to Start

When is the best time to start nurturing a dog? Various trainers believe in various times. For example, the Monks of New Skete, who train and sell German Shepherds, start picking up pups within a day after they're born. They explain that even though the puppies won't be able to hear or see for a while, they do know that they're being handled affectionately, and this sends them a very positive message–that they're valued and loved.

Other experts, such as Jean Craighead George, believe that socialization can start later; i.e., between of 4 and 13 weeks of age, but no later than that. She recommends that you make it a point to pick up the puppy every day, not only to handle her, but also to talk to her in a soothing, affectionate way. This will start you on the road to making the dog affectionate and responsive to you, and, in the end, a great candidate for training.

No matter how equally love is dispensed to each puppy in a litter, every dog will have individualistic characteristics that will make her different. For example, in wolf packs, some wolves are dominant and some are submissive. Understanding this concept can be important from a variety of points of view, especially when trying to choose the dog that's best suited for your lifestyle.

Alpha and Omega

Animal behaviorists call the most dominant wolf in the pack the "e" or "alpha," and the least dominant wolf the "omega." Dogs, believed to be the descendants of wolves, are also characterized this way.

Take your puppy with you wherever you go.

Alpha puppies will try to dominate their littermates.

Things You Can Tell Just by Looking at Them

How do you know which dog is an alpha and which is an omega? First, the alpha will be one of the largest animals in the pack. Also, when puppies play, the most dominant and least dominant will emerge. The alpha will show the most dominant behavior.

Alpha dogs also carry themselves a certain way, with their heads and tails up. Omega dogs show their position in the pack by putting their tails between their legs and lowering their heads when approached by the alpha.

You may not want an alpha dog–perhaps an omega or something in between in personality would work better. Your situation and your personality may work best with a dog that's easier to manage, for example, if you are an older person or if you work a lot. "An omega," says George, "makes a better dog for working people who do not have much time to interact with it. Omegas, which are often the smallest in their litter, are pleasant dogs, relatively nonaggressive, and often shy. Omegas make lovable pets. On the other hand, an alpha dog will do best in a family that admires its dominance, courage, initiative, persistence, and alertness."

Once you have the dog in your possession, the owner should be considered the alpha by the dog. As George says, "When you take a pup from its parents or adopt an adult, the dog turns its love of the leader upon you. It needs no reward for this gift other than praise and affection. It has one happiness–to please you. You do not have to strike your dog for doing wrong. Your frowns, finger shakes, and sharp words are enough." She goes on to say, "The more you behave like an alpha, the more smoothly the relationship will go."

Being an alpha is not a casual thing–it is a responsibility. The person who takes a puppy from her mother then becomes a member of the pack, and the dog will look to that person for leadership. Dog trainer Bashkim Dibra says, "It is vital for you to assume the alpha position in your dog's eyes immediately. Not only does your dog need your leadership in order to be secure and relaxed in the society of your home, but unless you seize the leadership (alpha) role

You should be the "alpha" in your relationship with your dog.

Aggression

Depending on the breed's inherent characteristics, some dogs may be aggressive to other dogs, animals, and people. This is something that should not be tolerated. Remember, you are the alpha, and if you don't squash such behavior immediately, it could become dangerous for yourself and other people, particularly if you are dealing with a large-breed dog.

However, you don't want to overreact to a dog's aggression, particularly if it is a dominant dog, by hitting her or threatening her. You want to correct her firmly by scolding her or otherwise disciplining her so that she knows that you are not challenging her, but are displeased. In other words, you are acting like a benevolent despot, a loving pack leader that must retain order. However, aggression is a problem that must be addressed and solved, if not through obedience training, then through professional assistance.

early in your relationship you will have a constant battle with your dog for dominance."

It should be made clear that one should not become tyrannical with a dog–dogs need to love you and bond with you in order to have a totally successful relationship. This won't happen if you are mean. However, the love you provide must be tough–it's okay to become a benevolent despot.

Your role as an alpha will continue for life of your dog, and she may challenge it, just as dogs will do to each other. When this occurs, you must quell the uprising immediately, or your authority may erode.

Tips for Being an Alpha

Following are some tips on assuming the alpha role in your relationship with your dog. First and foremost, praise her. Human beings need praise, not only because it helps us define what is acceptable behavior and what is not, but simply because it makes us feel good. Indeed,

Nurturing is very important to your pup's development.

the greatest leaders in history have been people who complement those who follow them.

Dogs also need praise to define their actions as acceptable and to make them feel good, which makes them desirous of pleasing their leader in the future.

When your dog does something right, she should be praised quickly and exuberantly, hands on, so

Praise is the key to training your puppy.

there will be no fuzziness about the message: You did a good job!

On the other hand, don't be excessive in your praise once she knows what the rules are. If she has responded well to a sit or heel command, let her know, but don't make it seem as if she were one of the Huskies that was part of the Itadarod run carrying life saving serum in the dead of winter.

Conversely, if the dog does something wrong, she should be corrected, but one should not go overboard. One "trainer" advocated beating the pup with a switch or putting her in a dark closet! An adequate correction may be a sharp pull on her leash and collar or a verbal correction– "No!" Then, when you complete the reprimand, give the dog a quick hug. This tells her that you still love her; it's just that you don't approve of this particular bit of behavior.

Also, when giving a command, you should make sure the dog does what you want the first time you say it. Don't repeat yourself.

Be prepared to praise or correct the dog immediately. For example, if your dog is running pell mell, you may bark out a command that she doesn't obey. Because you are not with her, you have no way to apply a correction. Only act if the dog is within correcting distance. Waiting until you catch her to punish her will only serve to confuse her. She will think she's being punished for coming to you.

A Puppy's Development

Like people, puppies go through various developmental stages. The following is what generally happens to a puppy, emotionally, physically, and psychologically, over the first ten weeks of life.

The First Two Weeks

A puppy is born blind and deaf, and for the first two weeks of her life, she doesn't do a lot except sleep (around 90 percent of the time) and eat. While she can't hear or see, she can feel and smell, and the combination enables her to find the all-important nipples on her mother. The mother dispenses milk that contains antibodies that help the pup survive for six to ten weeks. Propelling the pup to her mother are very undeveloped and weak legs. The puny legs also allow the puppy to huddle together with her siblings. The legs develop somewhat while the puppies are asleep because they twitch, something called "activated sleep."

These two-week-old pups depend on their mother for everything.

The puppy is nurtured by her mother, of course, which includes her mom licking her belly, which stimulates the little creature to defecate and urinate.

Depending on how the mother feels, human beings may or may not be allowed to pick up and nurture the puppies every day. When this occurs, it helps man and dog bond more easily.

The Third Week

During this week, the puppy's other senses start to operate. She can detect light and dark, as well as movement, and will respond to large or sudden sounds. She will start to interact with her brothers and sisters, and she starts developing social skills by this interaction, i.e., touching them with her paws and mouth.

Breeding only quality dogs ensures healthy, even-tempered puppies.

She learns to crawl, and her tail begins to wag. She can also venture from her mother to urinate on her own. In some cases, puppies, though not weaned, can be fed liquid food suggested by a veterinarian.

The Fourth and Fifth Weeks

During this period, the puppy's muscular development increases to the point where she can walk, run, and pounce on her littermates. It is a period of endless exploration, and the puppy's interaction with her siblings teaches her a lot, including when she's biting too hard–which elicits a tough response from a littermate–and where she belongs in the aristocracy of the pack–she will alternately sleep at the bottom and top of the puppy pile.

If the puppy is misbehaving, Mom occasionally may get involved by growling at her. This discipline sharpens the puppy's sense of right and wrong, which can make training easier. If dogs aren't subject to this kind of discipline, such as dogs who become orphaned, the human training process becomes that much more difficult.

Tales That Tails Tell

You can tell what a dog is thinking—or feeling—by observing the position of her tail. If straight out, she's wondering who is in charge. If it is in the upward position, it means that the dog feels she's the alpha and that she's important. A tail between the legs means that the dog feels badly about herself, is dominated by other dogs, or is depressed. If it is in a partially extended position with the tip turned up, it means that she may be ready to fight; a tail that's up and twisted a bit means she is definitely ready to fight.

And when a dog's tail is just normal position—down and loose—it means everything's okay.

Your puppy's mother will provide him with early discipline.

During this time, the puppy's teeth develop, and she may stop nursing. Around the fourth week, she can start eating food specially prepared by Mom, which is food she chews and swallows and then regurgitates.

The fourth week is usually the time when fear is developed: The puppy picks up her mother's fears and develops some of her own, including becoming afraid of her handler if she is treated poorly.

The latter portion of this time is when the puppy starts to become socialized with the human family, becoming more aware of the sights and sounds in the house, as well as interacting more with individual members.

The Sixth and Seventh Weeks

This is a time of wonder and curiosity for the young pup, but she is also very sensitive to emotional harm. Her emotions will be revealed; she'll start barking to get attention, whining to show fear, and whimpering if hurt. Take care not to scare or upset her in any way. It's best that the dog be allowed to relate one on one with a human being, allowing trust to start to build. It is also a time of great fun. She should be given a supply of toys, because she will be very rambunctious and needs them to interact. If she goes too far when playing, her mother will put her in her place. When the puppies are weaned, have their own teeth, and can eat by themselves, the mother dog assumes the role of alpha or pack leader. The mother will show her puppies–using toys–when it's appropriate to bite.

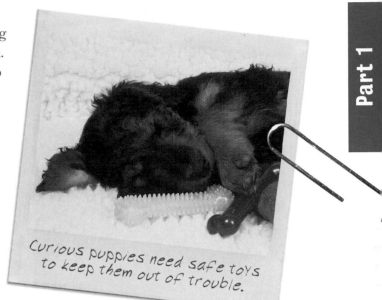

Curious puppies need safe toys to keep them out of trouble.

Puppies will also attack each other to establish dominance and to determine who is the alpha.

The Eighth Week

During the eighth week, the puppy will start to develop bathroom habits. She will use her own place to go, and it won't be near where she eats. She will search for a spot to urinate by sniffing around. The eighth week is also a crucial time in socialization–this is the time when fears can be established. You should take care to make sure that all the puppy's experiences are positive ones, or she may carry around the fear for life. It is best to wait until after the eighth week to take a puppy to her new home for this reason. For example, if the puppy gets carsick, she may be afraid of cars and it will take a lot of training and desensitization to get her to enjoy riding in one.

The breeder will start your puppy on the road to good nutrition.

Make sure all your puppy's experiences are positive.

The Tenth Week

Now the puppies stop battling each other—the alpha and omega in the litter have been established. This is the best time to get a sense of a puppy's personality. Any anxiety the puppy might have felt in a strange places ceases—she is ready to find a new home.

Key Points

• Nurturing—giving a dog hands-on love—is very important to its development.

• Socialization—exposing the dog to the world in general—is equally important.

• Nurturing by humans should begin as soon as the mother dog allows it.

• Some dogs are alphas (dominant) and some are omegas (submissive).

• An owner should automatically assume the role of alpha when he or she raises a dog.

• A good alpha applies tough love.

• Aggression must not be tolerated in a dog.

Part Two
Getting Ready

Try as he would, Joe never did get the hang of teaching his dog any tricks.

4

Supplies

Having the right supplies for your dog is important; some equipment enhances the quality of a dog's life, some are necessary for training. The following is a list of equipment that will serve you and your dog well.

Leash and Collar

You should get a leash and collar for your puppy, even if you expect to keep the dog in a fenced-in yard. A dog that is used to wearing a collar and leash is much easier to manage when you take him out, and they can be extremely helpful on visits to the veterinarian, if you are around other dogs or cats, or if there's an emergency.

There are many kinds of collars. The best kind to get for a puppy is one made of soft rolled leather or

Your puppy should get used to wearing a collar and leash.

ID tags will help your dog find his way home if he becomes lost.

Buy an adjustable nylon collar that can grow with your puppy.

nylon that buckles around the neck. Make sure you get a good quality one, or you'll have to replace it sooner. The size of the collar should be big enough for the puppy to grow into, but not so long that he trips over it or it hangs down. A collar with too much room could get caught on something and choke the puppy. The rule of thumb is that you should be able to fit three fingers in between the collar and the puppy's neck.

Do You Have ID?

The next thing to buy for your puppy after his leash and collar is an identification tag. These are very inexpensive and should be engraved with your last name, address, and phone number. This will increase the chances that your dog will be returned to you if he becomes lost.

Leashes are usually made of leather, webbed cotton or nylon, or chain link. The length of the leash should be six feet. I would avoid chain-link leashes, because they're too hard on the hands, even if you wear gloves.

Beware of Dog

Don't leave a puppy alone with a collar on. It could get entangled in something, and the puppy could accidentally choke himself.

Leather can also be hard on the digits, unless you wear gloves or soften the leather with softening agents. For these reasons, I prefer the webbed cotton. (There is also a chain-link type collar available, known as a "choke" training collar, but this is discussed later).

One of the essential lessons in a puppy's life is to learn to wear the collar and leash. Place the puppy in your lap, a safe place for him, and put the collar on, remembering,

At first, your puppy may resist walking on his lead.

Something Useful

A harness is useful in some situations. For example, a harness is used on Huskies that pull a sled or on Bloodhounds on the track (a collar might put restriction in their neck), but it doesn't work as a training aid. It can be used, however, once a dog is trained or to take pressure off its neck if it develops back or joint problems.

as suggested earlier, to allow three fingers of space between the collar and neck. You should constantly offer him reassurance throughout the exercise.

Gently place the puppy on the floor and observe him. Some pups will do nothing, some will try to shake off the collar, and some will get a little panicky and attempt to get it off by pawing or biting. If the last scenario occurs, by all means take the collar off and repeat the exercise the next day.

When the puppy is used to wearing the collar, it's time for the leash. Just snap it on and then let the puppy track it around as he wishes. After a while, loop the end of the leash over a doorknob or some other item that gives the puppy the sensation of being restrained. At first—or second—he may fight it, but soon he will sit or lie down, resigned to the fact that he's not going anywhere.

Toys

Toys are necessary equipment for puppies, not only to let them exercise safely, but also to teethe properly—and not do their teething on the leg of your favorite ottoman.

Special harnesses can be purchased for adult dogs.

Part 2

With patience, your pup will walk with you.

Just as you would exercise care in selecting toys for a child, do the same for your puppy. Do not buy toys that can come apart or splinter, or toys have small parts that can be swallowed and choke the dog. Other no-nos include toys that have sharp points or attachments, such as sneakers; balls of string, cellophane, yarn, twist ties, small plastic bags, (which can also choke a puppy), as well as things that it might be able to pull apart, such as toys made of sponge rubber, fur, or wool. These may be swallowed and wreak havoc on the digestive tract. In general, if a puppy can put his jaws around the toy, it's too small.

Chewable, edible bones made especially for puppies, like those made by Nylabone®, are great and help your puppy's teeth stay clean and healthy.

Housing

When you bring a puppy home, it's a good idea to have already decided where he is going to live and to have the area set up and ready for him.

If he is to stay outside the house part of the time, then he must be provided with a doghouse that protects him from the cold. Certain dogs can tolerate quite a bit of cold, but if the dog is kept indoors most of the year and then outdoors the other part, his body will not be attuned to very cold weather. Also, smaller breeds or short-coated breeds do not well outside in the cold for long periods of time.

Provide your puppy with an assortment of safe toys.

Provide a house that's just big enough so that the puppy or dog can heat it with his own body heat. An ideal size is a house that's slightly bigger than a dog when it's curled up. For example, if the dog

How Are Dogs Affected by Cold?

There is a general view that dogs have a built-in protection against cold. This is not true and, depending on the breed, they may need separate garments to help them stay warm in frigid temperatures. The short-haired breeds, such as the Doberman Pinscher and the Dachshund, need to don a sweater during cold weather. Sweaters are available at pet store or by mail order—to obtain the proper size sweater, measure the dog from neck to the base of the tail.

were a Cocker Spaniel, you wouldn't want to provide it with a house big enough for a German Shepherd.

Insulation is great for a house inhabited by human beings but not good for a doghouse, unless the climate is very cold. Insulation helps keep heat inside the house– perhaps too much heat. Humidity can rise, condensation can form, and the dog can get colder or become more susceptible to disease.

The doghouse should be built facing your house and should have a removable roof for easier cleaning. The roof should be only an inch or two higher than the standing dog's back, and the roof itself should have only a slight pitch for rain runoff. Many dogs like to go on the roof to sun themselves or get a better view of their territory.

The door should have a windbreak, such as a heavy piece of cloth or other flexible material. One good ready-made doghouse is a barrel with a hole in the front. If you own a larger doghouse already, you can just place the barrel inside the house. As the puppy gets

Provide a comfortable place for your pup to retreat.

Make your yard escape-proof to keep your dog safe.

Part 2

In the Doghouse

If you decide to build a doghouse for your dog, make sure you measure carefully. I know of one man who built a doghouse for his pooch of the finest materials and covered it in siding and roofing material that reflected those on his own house. The only problem was that the dog was too big to stand up in it without taking the roof off!

A fence will keep your dog in and other dogs out.

bigger, you can install a bigger barrel. In any case, you should mount the barrel on bricks, wood, or other material that prevents it from rolling. The floor should be lined with a washable blanket of some sort.

In the summer or in areas where weather is always mild or warm, doghouse dimensions don't matter. To get relief from the heat, a dog will simply lie outside under the stars. Just make sure he has a shady spot to retreat to during the daytime.

Containing the Dog

If you have the right kind of fencing, you may choose to let your dog have the run of the yard, and provide a doghouse to retreat to in case of rain.

Another way to confine you dog in a yard is with a wire fence enclosure or a dog run. This should be high enough so that the dog can't jump over it. For most breeds, this means it should be at least five feet high. For outstanding jumpers like Dobermans and German Shepherds, six feet should be adequate. The run should be big enough so that your dog has room to move around comfortably.

You may erect a fence for a puppy, but it should be designed to accommodate the dog when he grows older, and it should be strong enough to keep other dogs out. For this reason, the bottom of the wire should be buried at least eight inches underground. A stronger arrangement is to mount the fence on a concrete slab whose bottom goes below the frost line (i.e., the point at with the ground freezes solid) and eight inches above the ground, with the bottom of the fencing attached to the top of the slab. Make sure you provide shelter within the dog run in case of bad weather.

Living Inside

A dog should have a bed of his own where he can retreat to sleep, grab naps, escape from the kids, and store his toys, balls, and other playthings. Having a place to call his own is a helpful device in housetraining, because of the puppy's reluctance to urinate or defecate where he lives.

For a puppy, a crate can make an excellent temporary home. Size is important; you don't want to have your pup feel dwarfed by the crate, so either buy a puppy-sized crate, or if you buy an adult-sized one, place a partition in it so the space is cut down and the puppy feels surrounded. Get a good-quality crate and line it with a soft, washable material.

A crate makes an excellent home for your puppy.

Part 2

You can also use a dog pen lined with a blanket instead of a crate as a bed. Again, the size of the pen will vary according to the dog's size. If the dog is small, like a Chihuahua, the pen can be small–three feet square is fine. But if the dog is larger, like a Saint Bernard, make the pen large enough for him to be comfortable.

The pen can be very simple, made from a sheet of plywood or a wood frame with chicken wire stapled to it. Or, if you wish, you can buy a pen from a pet store. A variety of enclosures are available.

A bed should go inside the pen or crate. The bed can be a small box with soft bedding (a pillow, cloth, etc.), or you can buy one of a variety of beds at a pet store. Do not to get a bed made of chewable material like wicker, because a puppy can swallow pieces of it. Whatever bedding you choose, the enclosure should be big enough to allow the puppy to lie down. Puppies like the feeling of being surrounded by walls.

You can also segment off a section of the kitchen or bathroom to create a puppy home. The kitchen or the bathroom is the best place for your puppy, because the floors are usually made of easily cleaned material, like tile or linoleum. Baby gates can be helpful in sectioning of a small area for your puppy to stay in.

Sturdy bowls will keep your dog and your floors clean.

Food and Water Bowls

The bowls that you buy for your puppy's food and water should be the kind that will not tip over.

If you wish, you can buy puppy-size bowls to guard against your pet falling in and going for an unscheduled swim or scuba dive through the food. Any bowl you buy should also be easy to clean–stainless steel is very good.

Key Points

• Your puppy should become used to wearing a leash and collar.

• Get an identification tag for your dog's collar.

• Don't leave a puppy alone with a collar around his neck.

• Safe chew toys are necessary to your puppy's development.

• Have a place for your puppy to sleep inside before you bring him to his new home.

• Crates are very useful tools for housebreaking your new puppy. They also provide a safe place for him to retreat.

5

Nutrition

A number of years ago, after reading the ingredients on a can of dog food, David Letterman snidely commented that his dog "Bob" didn't pay much attention to ingredients, spending "much of his day with his nose in the toilet or the garbage."

As funny as this is, any dog would be a lot better off if his owner was more concerned with his diet. He'd live longer, have more energy, and be less susceptible to disease, just as his human counterparts are when they adhere to a good diet.

A plentiful supply of good food will keep your dog healthy and happy, and a happy dog is far easier to control than an unhappy one.

There are many brands of dog food from which to choose.

Dog Food

Today, approximately ten billion dollars is spent on dog and cats, and the bulk of that money is spent buying food. There are some 34 million dogs in the US–that adds up to a lot of food.

Dog food comes in three different forms: dry, canned, and semi-moist, and it is estimated that there are 15,000 different dog foods on the market. Many are regional brands, but many are made for national markets.

The food comes in a wide variety of shapes and sizes, resembling everything from bones to steaks. It varies greatly in cost, too. Dried dog food is cheaper than canned or semi-moist. It is estimated that to feed dry food to a mid-sized dog, it would cost around one dollar a day, while canned food costs two or three dollars, a sum that can add up over a year. When you buy canned food, you also should know that only 25 percent of the contents is food; the other 75 percent is water. Nutritionally, dry dog food is just as good as moist.

If you asked a dog who had never had either canned or dry food which type he'd prefer (and we can't verify this), it would probably be the canned kind. Canned food has a stronger smell than dry food, and is, of course, closer to what a dog, a descendant of the wolf, would eat.

However, dry dog food, in addition to costing less, is easier to manage. You can pour out a bowl full of food, and leave it there for a period of time, the dog will eat it as he wishes. If you do the same thing with canned dog food, it can attract bacteria that can make a dog sick.

Myths About Nutrition

There are a number of myths concerning what dogs should and should not eat.

√ Milk is a good environment for worms. If this were true, why wouldn't it cause worms in people?

√ Bones are required for good teeth. In fact, it's not the bones themselves, that are important, but the elements that make them up. Ground bone is an ingredient found in all nutritiously prepared foods.

√ Meat makes dogs vicious.

√ Cooked meat is better for a dog than raw. In fact, a dog can survive very nicely on raw, dried, or cooked meat—or no meat at all.

√ Dogs cannot digest potatoes. Dogs gulp their food and will gulp down chunks of potatoes with no ill effects. Puppies can also eat potatoes, but they should be given in mashed form.

√ Fats cannot be digested. In fact, a dog can absorb up to 70 percent of the fat in their diet, and no diet with less than 15 percent fat can be considered balanced.

√ Garlic kills worms in food.

The Nose Knows

How efficient is a dog's nose? In a word, he's a superstar. Some scientists have said that a dog's ability to detect odors is 100 times better than a human being's, while others estimate it at a million times or more. This ability is related to number of olfactory cells in the nose: Humans have about 5 million; a dog has 220 million.

The dog's sense of smell seems to depend, however, on what the dog is seeking to smell. For example, it can identify human sweat up to six weeks after a person has touched an object very briefly. A Bloodhound can pick up a scent that has been imparted through feet with shoes on for four days and can track that scent for up to a hundred miles.

Dry food can help keep your dog's teeth clean.

One other advantage of dry food is that a dog will get to use his teeth more actively while chewing it, thus scraping off any built-up tartar.

Some people are concerned that dry dog food is not satisfying, but once you establish your dog on dry food, he will be fine, as demonstrated every day by most veterinary hospitals, kennels, and breeding farms that prefer it over canned. It is also okay to moisten the dry food with some canned dog food if you wish.

Variety is Not the Spice of Life

Don't worry about your dog getting variety in his diet—that doesn't matter to a dog. What he likes, he likes. In fact, if you change foods midstream, you may pay for it. In his book, *Good Owners, Great Dogs,* dog expert Brian Kilcommons tells about a Miniature Schnauzer that was brought to him with a nonstop barking problem, something unusual because this breed of dog is not usually a barker.

Kilcommons solved the mystery when he learned that the problem began three weeks before when the owner had changed the brand of the dog food. The owner returned to the usual brand and the dog stopped barking instantly.

A healthy adult dog should be fed once a day.

A healthy adult dog should be fed once a day. If you feed dry food exclusively, and your dog has not consumed all of the food in one sitting, empty it out and add just enough to the dish to equal the discarded portion.

A common problem overfeeding. You shouldn't rely on dog food labels–these commonly recommended portions that are too large, and if you adhere to them, you'll end up with a dog that needs to go to on a diet. Your best bet on this subject–and any other food questions–is to check with your veterinarian.

In addition to canned or dry food, some table scraps can be included in dog's diet, including meat, cottage cheese, bread, cooked eggs, and milk (in small amounts). The amount of table scraps should never be equal to the amount of dry food a dog gets, because this will spoil his appetite for the dry food, just like giving a child a piece of cake before his dinner would spoil his appetite.

You don't need to buy special, premium dog food to ensure that your dog will like the taste or that he is getting all the nutrients he needs. Tests of premium versus lower-priced foods

Pudgy Pooch?

Like people, dogs are subject to putting on extra pounds. One way to test if your dog is overweight is to try to feel his ribs. If you can't feel the ribs, the dog is past a healthy weight. You should also be able to see a waistline beneath the rib cage when you look at the animal from above. You may think the situation is simply remedied by feeding the dog less, but this can result in a begging assault on your sensibilities that you'll have to constantly resist, or a food-stealer that can't be trusted at the dinner table.

To deal with the problem, here are a few strategies: If you are feeding the dog table scraps, cease and desist. In addition to feeding him less, exercise him more, just as you would if you expected to lose weight. If your dog is grossly overweight, it is best to consult with a veterinarian on how to lose the extra pounds. The vet may suggest that you feed the dog a lower-calorie food that isn't sold in standard outlets.

Nutrition Levels

Some dog food brands are more nutritious than others. Some contain more cereal than is desirable. To determine the quality of the dog food, check the ingredient list on the package. Ingredients are listed according to amount: the greatest amount, first; the second greatest, second; and so forth. If you see cereal grains listed first, second, and third, chances are the dog food is indeed mostly cereal, which is not nutritious.

indicated no preference for the high-priced stuff.

Check the Label

You should check the label on the dog food that you purchase to make sure that it complies with the nutrients required by the Association of American Feed Control Officials (AAFCO), a nonprofit group of federal and state officials. The standards are printed on the labels of foods that comply.

Checking this label is important and sometimes surprising. One consumer magazine that studied dog and cat food found that a quarter of the dog foods were lacking in calcium, which is a bone builder, and potassium, which is needed for nerves and metabolic processes to function properly.

The premium dog foods may have one advantage over the lower-priced brands. Portions that are the same size have more calories, and while nutritionally complete, can lead to stools that are smaller, drier, and easier to handle—a good thing in areas where there are "pooper scooper" laws. Also, you don't need to buy the higher-priced "light" or "lean" foods, because they may not have lower calories and less fat than lower-priced brands.

Treats should be a nutritious part of your dog's regular diet.

Buy a food that is formulated for your dog's stage of life.

Part 2

A dog should not be fed highly spiced, greasy, or fried foods, or foods with sharp bones such as fish, pork, and poultry. Sharp bones can cause cuts or perforations in the stomach and bowel. Even potato chips are a no-no for dogs– some do not chew their food and the chips, which go down whole, retain their sharp edges and points, which can do damage to delicate intestinal linings and cause pain strong enough to produce convulsions.

Like people, dogs can suffer digestive problems from certain foods. Foods that classically cause problems are eggs, milk, corn, and soy products.

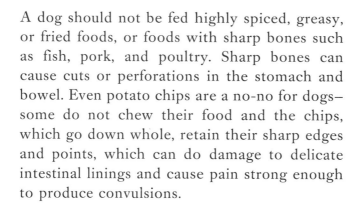

The Good Old Days

Years ago, people didn't worry much about feeding a dog food that was good for it. The usual procedure was to look down at the dog's pleading eyes and dump the meat scraps on everyone's plate into his bowl. While there's nothing wrong with table scraps, a steady diet of meat is not a balanced diet. Indeed, in the wild, nature takes care of the nutritional balance with canines that eat not only meat, but also bones, stomach contents of prey, and wild fruits and grasses.

Feeding Schedule

In general, feeding a dog twice a day works out nicely, though once a day is the traditional practice. Your best bet is to consult with your vet. The im-portant point is to be consistent. Consistency in feeding times helps you in two respects: Your dog will always know when its time to eat, and you'll have a much better idea of when he will need to go outside to eliminate.

Feeding Bowls

Feeding bows are made of metal, ceramic, and plastic. I prefer either of the first two because they are easy to clean and sturdy. Plastic bowls are okay, except they seem to be guilty of changing the color of a dog's nose, with coloration passing from the plastic, giving it a speckled look. They also are more like to split, and bacteria can form in the cracks. Plastic bowls also make convenient chew toys for mischievous teething puppies.

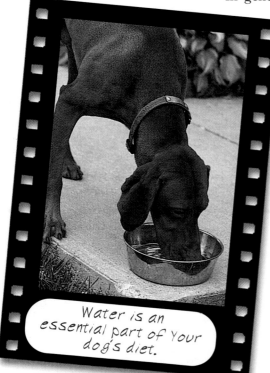

Water is an essential part of your dog's diet.

Bowls come in various depths and widths, and some are handier for dogs of different facial dimensions to use. A little investigation should reveal what's right for you and your dog.

If you want to make things easier at dinnertime, you can build or buy a little platform to set the bowls on, so the dog doesn't have to stretch his neck so much.

Key Points

• More expensive brands of dog food are not necessarily better than less expensive brands. Dry food, though cheaper, is just as good as canned or semi-moist food, and dogs can learn to like dry food easily.

• Don't make the mistake of feeding a dog too much. Follow your veterinarian's recommendations for portion sizes and watch your dog's weight carefully.

• Some dog foods are more nutritious then others. Brands with a lot of cereals as their main ingredients are no good. Check the label for the AAFCO seal of approval.

• Dog foods labeled "premium" are not necessarily better for your dog. Regular dog food, as long as it has the approval of AAFCO, is fine.

• Don't feed a dog greasy food, table scraps, or food with sharp edges.

• Feed an adult dog once or twice a day, depending on your schedule.

Provide your dog with cool clean water, especially when outside.

Good nutrition will be evident in your dog's healthy appearance.

6

Health and Grooming

Health Care

A huge Mastiff named "Pete" was trying his best to lie down, but every time he did, he got up right away. His belly, large to begin with, seemed a bit distended. Luckily for Pete, his owner was alert to the symptoms of bloat, a gastrointestinal condition that can be fatal, and immediately called the veterinarian. Upon hearing the symptoms, the vet told the owner to rush Pete in for emergency treatment. The owner did, and as a result, Pete lived; however, if he had not gotten immediate treatment, he may have died.

Having a general knowledge of your dog's health should be every bit as important to the owner as the health of other family members. This knowledge can

Owners should have a general knowledge of their dog's health.

Breed Concerns

In addition to the diseases mentioned here, there are some other maladies that are breed specific. Most mid-sized and small-sized dogs, such as terriers and Toy breeds, are very hardy and long lived, while most of the larger dogs, such as Great Danes, are short lived and are prone to bloat and hip dysplasia, an abnormality of the hip joint that can cripple a dog.

Most of the Toy breeds are sensitive to heat and cold and are prone to a malady called slipped stifle, which is a dislocation of the kneecap.

Breeds that have bulging eyes, such as Pugs, fall victim to eye lacerations and respiratory and heart ailments, while dogs with big droopy ears are subject to ear infections.

Eye problems are more prevalent in dogs with protruding eyes.

help to save your dog's life someday, but it also impacts on how a dog is trained and handled.

Also, certain breeds are subject to certain maladies, and with this knowledge, you can be on the lookout for problems.

Allergies

Like people, dogs are subject to a variety of allergies. Finding out what is causing the problem is certainly a job for a vet, although careful observation by the owner can be very helpful. For example, owners noticed that their dog only seemed to have allergic reactions when she was at home. Whenever she was out of the house for any length of time—something that occurred fairly frequently because they traveled—the problem ceased. The vet was unsuccessful in making a diagnosis.

The answer finally came when the owners read an article about mold causing allergic reactions. They had the house probed by a company that specialized in airborne mold, and a startling discovery was made: A thick, grayish mold had taken up residence in the ducts of the heating/cooling system and was being spewed out in the air. When the dog breathed this air, she had an allergic reaction. The firm cleaned out the ducts, and the problem went away.

Other causes for allergic reactions may be perfume, carpet fresheners, cigarette smoke, plants, room deodorizers, and food, even foods the dog has been eating without a problem for years.

Part 2

Symptoms

You should become familiar with symptoms that may signify the common diseases that can impact your dog. The following are symptoms that could have some medical significance and should trigger a call to your vet.

√ Thirstier than usual	√ Can't lie down easily
√ Swollen tongue	√ Wheezes
√ Loss of appetite	√ Blood in urine
√ Eats but doesn't gain weight	√ Drools too much
√ Yellowish eyes	√ Rubs backside on ground
√ Scratches excessively	√ Lesions on skin
√ Fur has bald patches or fur is matted, dull, or sparse	√ Keeps walking in circles
	√ Bites at air
√ Has difficulty defecating	√ Vomits excessively
√ Has difficulty urinating	√ Ears swollen
√ Shivers when it's not cold	√ Pupils are dilated
√ Has bad breath	√ Eyes dull or bloodshot
√ Pants, breathing is rapid and shallow	√ Shakes head constantly
√ Stomach looks distended	√ Ears smell

Though individual causes may be hard to find, there are general symptoms that can point to allergies. (One of the more interesting causes was noted by animal expert Jack Hanna. He said that some dogs can respond allergically to a single flea.) Usually, allergies manifest as skin problems–itching, scratching, biting the skin, excessive licking, dandruff, and scabs.

Eyes may tear and turn red from conjunctivitis, and the dog may sneeze.

You can help prevent allergies by making fleas unwelcome in your home. In the past, pet owners had to bomb the house with insecticide

Dogs are subject to a variety of allergies.

Certain foods may cause your dog to have an allergic reaction.

Dogs can pick up fleas or ticks from playing outside.

to clear it of fleas, but today vets have powerful but safe medications that make this unnecessary. Keeping the dog properly groomed, including regular brushing and bathing, also tends to take in the welcome mat for fleas.

Bad Backs

A variety of things can cause back problems. One problem is called invertebral disc lesions. This malady is common to long-backed breeds such as the Dachshund, Cocker Spaniel, and Pekingese. At the core of the problem is a protruding spinal disc, which applies pressure to the spinal cord.

The symptoms may present themselves when the dog is jumping off of something or running. She may become lame, even paralyzed in the hind legs, and you'll notice that she doesn't stand or walk, because she doesn't have the use of her rear legs. She may also go into a position with her legs out behind her like a frog.

The answer to the problem is back surgery, which is usually successful, and with the help of medication and her owner's care, the dog is usually fine.

Bloat

When a dog exhibits any of the symptoms associated with this disease, it requires immediate emergency care. Symptoms include dry heaves, a high degree of restlessness, drooling, and a swollen or distended belly. The condition, which is technically known as gastric dilation-torsion, can be fatal.

Although the exact cause of bloat is unknown, it is thought to be caused by the dog gulping food or water and exercising at the wrong time, especially right after eating. It usually affects large-chested breeds, like the Great Dane or the Mastiff. To help prevent bloat, it's a good idea to limit water intake after feeding and never exercise your dog immediately after meals.

Parvovirus

I had a cat that had parvo, and I can't remember the experience without a certain squeezing sensation in my stomach. When I took "Oreo" to the vet, he examined him and announced that he had the virus. He stated that my options were to either put him down or watch him die.

Being a stubborn type, as well as a writer who had learned not to believe everything I heard, I researched the disease and finally got some advice on treating it from a research vet at the Cornell School of Veterinary medicine. Oreo survived, and I got myself a new vet.

Canine parvovirus is just as nasty. It can kill your dog. Its symptom includes diarrhea, listlessness, and loss of weight. Parvovirus is spread by contaminated feces, which can unknowingly be carried from place to place on car tires, shoes, and, of course, pet paws.

Vaccination is the only way to ensure that your dog does not catch this disease.

Diabetes

The pancreas produces insulin to balance the amount of sugar in the blood, and when it doesn't, sugar builds up and causes diabetes. As such, an animal is subject to the same possible complications as people, including loss of sight and limbs.

Dogs like the Dachshund can suffer from back problems.

Vaccinations will keep your puppy safe from disease.

Part 2

Part 2

To guard against diabetes, feed your dog so that she maintains a desired weight (heavier dogs are more prone to the disease) and resist the impulse to feed her candy or treats high in sugar.

Distemper

This is a dangerous viral disease that can be fatal and can be spread with airborne contact. It comes from the excretions of wild animals and dogs. Symptoms include yellow discharge from the eyes and nose, listlessness, coughing, vomiting, and twitching muscles.

To guard against it, have your pup inoculated at six weeks or when the vet suggests, and get booster shots as recommended.

Ear Infections

A dog with an ear infection frequently shakes her head, and a foul odor may emanate from one or both ears. Mites may also cause a problem; these are characterized by redness or dirt in the ears.

To guard against infection, clean your dog's ears regularly with an ear cleaner and take her to the veterinarian immediately if she shows any of the above-mentioned symptoms.

Heartworm

Heartworm is caused by mosquitoes that are infected with parasites. Symptoms include lethargy, coughing, and weight loss. This condition is frequently fatal. To guard against it, have your dog tested for the condition and ask your vet for heartworm-prevention pills. It's also a good idea to keep her from areas where there are mosquitoes, if possible.

Puppies can pick up diseases from other dogs.

Keep your dog's ears clean and dry to prevent infection.

Hookworms

Hookworms reside in soil containing the feces of pets infected with the disease. Hookworms can be prevented by keeping the areas that the dog uses clean and by washing your hands after handling.

Hookworms are a disease that a dog and other pets can transmit to humans, and that is one reason why it is so important to pick up after your dog.

Kennel Cough

If you have to put your pooch in a kennel for a while, by all means have her inoculated against kennel cough before her stay. This respiratory disease is characterized by a dry, hacking cough and is caused by dogs passing a viral infection from one to another.

Leptospirosis

Veterinarians consider leptospirosis to be one of the most dangerous diseases that a dog can contract because it is contagious, it can be caught by humans, and can leave either the dog or the person with weakened kidneys or a weak heart.

The cause of the disease is a spiral-shaped bacterium that is thought to be spread through contact with dog or rat urine. Dogs that roam outside are susceptible to catching it, but it seems to attack the short-legged dogs more than long-legged ones, because it can enter though the penis or vulva, something that more likely to happen if the animal is closer to the ground. There are two forms of the

As your dog matures, annual checkups are necessary to ensure good health.

Keeping your yard clean is the best preventative against parasites.

Excessive scratching can indicate a skin problem.

disease. One, technically known as *leptospira icteromorrhagica,* is the more serious form and can cause hemorrhaging and jaundice in dogs and Weil's disease in man. The other form is milder and is often not diagnosed correctly because its symptoms are more difficult to track.

In the milder form, the puppy's temperature often elevates to 103 degrees or more. Symptoms include urine that ranges in color from dark yellow to brown, congested eyes, vomiting, diarrhea, loose stools, and difficulty moving.

The more serious form of the disease includes the same symptoms but turns the whites of the eyes and the skin yellow, and the interior lips orange. There may be blood in the stools, and blood may be vomited.

Vaccination is key to guarding against this disease. A vet can vaccinate your puppy against both the severe and mild forms. The disease can be treated with antibiotics. If the heart or kidneys have been damaged, however, symptoms won't show up until the dog is middle aged.

Lyme Disease
This is a relatively modern disease, but it's a serious one that causes anemia, as well as paralysis and death. Certain kinds of ticks carry Lyme disease. When you groom your dog, note if any ticks are present. If they are, pull them straight out with a pair of tweezers. If you live in an area where there is a heavy concentration of ticks, ask your vet if he can vaccinate or provide some other form of protection for your dog.

Mange
This is a disease that attacks the skin, causing redness, dandruff, loss of hair, and itching.

Mites are the culprits. Thoroughly grooming your dog is the best way to prevent mange. If you live in an area where mites are a particular problem, ask your vet if there are any special preventatives against them.

Snake Bites

"If you live in the city," says one veterinarian, "your worries relate more to moving vehicles than snakes, but if you live in the country, then snakebites can be a concern."

While snakebites are a concern, they are not necessarily fatal. Not all snakes are poisonous. Many, such as garter snakes, king snakes, and bull snakes, will bite, but with no more effect than a puncture to your skin.

Other snakes–rattlesnakes, coral snakes, copperheads, and water moccasins–can cause damage if their bite transmits poison. However, studies have shown that half of all snake bites by supposedly poisonous snakes do not, for one reason or another, transmit the poison. Of course, if your dog is bitten by a snake, you should assume that the snakebite is dangerous.

If your dog is bitten and you are not sure what kind of snake did it, capture the snake (if you can) and bring it to the vet; the vet can dovetail the course of treatment depending on the type of snake it is. (Of course, in catching the snake, take care that you don't get bitten yourself.) If your dog is bitten, get her to a vet right away. Don't do any first aid yourself. Carry her in if she's not too heavy. The vet will administer a variety of medications such as antivenin, fluids, cortisone, antibiotics, and tetanus shots.

A basic knowledge of first aid can save your dog's life.

Tonsillitis

While tonsillitis is frequently thought of as a childhood disease and associated with copious amounts of ice cream, the disease occurs frequently in dogs and may be a one-time origin or a chronic condition. Symptoms include gagging, coughing, and vomiting. The dog will often act lethargic, have no appetite, run a fever, and be generally out of sorts. Often you can feel one or both of the tonsils, which will be swollen, by putting your hand just below the jaw.

You may have to give your dog medication if he is ill.

Good health care will be reflected in your dog's appearance.

The disease is often caused by a bacterial infection, coming from infected anal glands that the dog licks, and the bacteria enter the mouth.

Caught early, tonsillitis is easy to cure; the veterinarian will give the dog a broad-spectrum antibiotic, as well as a cortisone shots to reduce the swelling of the tonsils.

Like children, dogs will benefit greatly from being fed cold foods like ice cream, milk, and cold broth. Such items help soothe the throat and encourage the dog to eat other foods to get his energy up. However, check with your vet first and fed the dog whatever diet the vet recommends.

If a dog experiences chronic tonsillitis without any infection in the anal glands, then surgical removal of the tonsils is often the best way to proceed.

Rabies

Who can forget Cujo? In the movie based on the book by Stephen King, Cujo suffered from rabies and would have eventually died. The problem for his victims, of course, was that he didn't die soon enough.

Cujo could have been vaccinated against rabies, but this wouldn't have helped the drama!

At any rate, people can catch rabies, and getting a dog vaccinated against the disease is a very good idea, not to mention a law in almost all the states in the US.

Worms

If a dog is exhibiting any of the symptoms listed previously, she may be suffering from some form of worms. There are various kinds of these intestinal parasites. The vet can determine what kind they are by examining a stool sample.

Worms can be dangerous. Roundworms get in the intestines and the lungs and can cause death. Hookworms cause anemia in puppies and dogs; whipworms cause a loss of conditioning in a puppy, while tapeworms can make the stomach distend. Once the vet has identified the particular type of worm, he can treat it with various medications.

Hazardous Substances

One night when they were ready to go to bed, Tod and Bonnie Dawson called for their three dogs: Maverick, a German Wirehaired Pointer, and Madonna and Elia, two Lhasa Apsos. They didn't come. Bonnie investigated and found the dogs in another area of the house, their tails wagging furiously, and strewn around them were the remains of what had been a two-pound box of chocolates.

Choosing a reputable, caring vet will help your pet to feel more comfortable.

Emergency Treatment

If your dog has ingested something she shouldn't, you can call the National Animal Poison Control Center's (NAPCC) 24-hour hotline (1-800-548-2423) to get advice (at this writing there is a $45 fee for the service), or you can bring the dog to a local vet or emergency clinic. If the substance came in some sort of container, by all means be ready to read the contents off the label. This can help the vet advise you on what to do.

Keep calm. Your dog may be confused and upset, and your calmness will help her. It can be helpful to have materials needed to make a dog vomit. You can use one teaspoon of hydrogen peroxide or one teaspoon of salt or mustard powder in a cup of warm water, and place it on the back of the dog's tongue.

You should not try to make the dog vomit if she is unconscious, in shock, or has swallowed a substance that can burn on its way out of the dog, such as alkalis, petroleum solvents, acids, or a sharp object.

Baby gates can keep your dog from dangers in your home.

It was not a comical scene to Bonnie, who knew that chocolate could be very harmful to dogs, causing irregular heartbeat and seizures, even death.

Bonnie called the National Animal Poison Control Center (NAPCC), and after talking with their experts, she was counseled to get the dogs in for emergency treatment immediately. She did, and the story had a happy ending. All the dogs survived because the vets were able to induce vomiting by placing apomorphine under the dogs' eyelids, which activates the nausea center in the brain.

It was lucky that the Dawsons knew about the danger of chocolate. Indeed, if a 20-pound dog ingested only three ounces of baker's chocolate, it would be enough to kill her, because it contains caffeine and a substance called theobromine.

Other Hazards

To keep your pooch out of harm's way, be aware of other dangers:

• Don't tie up a dog that is wearing a choke-chain collar.

• Don't leave your dog in a car on a hot day, even with the windows cracked for ventilation. Temperatures inside a car can easily climb above 100 degrees when the weather is relatively mild.

• Don't leave your dog in a RV for a long time, even with the air conditioning on. If the power fails, the RV could heat up to dangerous levels.

• Don't use a prong or pinch collar on a puppy.

Keep a close eye on your puppy while he is outdoors.

Beware-for Dog

Chocolate is just one of a number of substances that can be upsetting, harmful, or dangerous to dogs. Other things include:

√ Onions

√ Onion powder

√ Yeast dough

√ Toothpaste—It may seem like a good idea to brush your pooch's teeth with toothpaste made for humans, but you shouldn't do it. Unlike people, a dog can't spit out the toothpaste and when he swallows it, it can cause stomach upset.

√ Antifreeze—This is like arsenic to a dog—less than one tablespoonful could kill a 20-pound dog. Antifreeze has a sweet odor, so keep it locked up or in a place where your dog can't get at it. When out walking your dog, avoid the greenish puddles you may find in the driveway or in the street.

√ Mouse or rat poison—Make sure that your dog does not eat mouse or rat poison or a dead rodent that may have died from ingesting one of these poisons.

√ Pesticides and household chemicals

√ Health and beauty products, such as deodorants, hair spray, nail polish, etc.

√ Tobacco—Cigarettes, cigars, etc. contain nicotine, which is hazardous to a dog's health.

√ Small bones—Like a baby chewing on small toy parts, a dog can choke on small bones. They can also cause intestinal blockages.

√ Medication—Medicine may be good for you, but it is lethal for your dog. That great anti-pain drug ibuprofen, for example, can cause stomach ulcers and kidney failure. If a dog ingests enough, it can cause coma or death.

√ Plants—Some plants can cause upset stomach, tremors, depression, and death. The most common poisonous plants are: aloe, tulip, iris, yew plant, oleander, hyacinth, sago palm, castor bean, rhododendron, daffodil, and lily.

• Keep your dog's head inside a car when it's moving. When your dog sticks her head out the window of a moving car, she could get injured, debris could get in her eye, or she could get an ear infection.

• Don't let your pooch play with matches. She can't start a fire, but matches, even the safety kind, contain phosphorous, which is poisonous.

• Wipe down paws after winter or wet-weather walks, because road salt and anti-icing materials can coat a dog's paws. They are poisonous, and if a dog licks them off, it can kill him. Also, wet paws can lead to bacterial infections.

Grooming

Dogs need to be groomed, and as smart as some of them are, the day has not arrived yet when this is a do-it-yourself job. You, as an owner, need to add grooming to your list of regular activities with your dog, not only to keep her looking good, but to keep her feeling good as well. Basic grooming consists of caring for a dog's coat and nails, and anything else required depends on the breed of dog and type of coat she has.

Brushing

All dogs shed to one degree or another. If you brush or comb your dog's coat

Check your dog's paws for injuries after walking outside.

Accidents

If your dog is in an accident, don't leave him alone. The dog will be frightened, and his instinct will be to run away, which can worsen injuries and delay what is perhaps life-saving treatment.

Cover the dog with a blanket. This helps preserve his body heat and avoid shock. Carry him on a flat board or similar item and muzzle him: A friendly dog that's scared and in pain may bite the hand that's trying to save him.

If the animal is bleeding, place a bandage on the wound and apply pressure. If necessary, tie a tourniquet above the wound to stop bleeding, loosening it every five minutes or so. Then get your dog to the nearest emergency animal hospital.

Part 2

frequently enough, shedding is not a real problem. Most breeds shed or "blow" their entire coat once or twice a year, while other breeds, such as the German Shepherd and Dalmatian, shed all year round.

Other breeds shed minimally, and some breeds, like the Poodle, hardly shed at all (but Poodles need to be trimmed regularly). Long hair will be more difficult to get off clothing or other cloth items than short hair, and white and light hairs are usually easier to spot than dark hairs.

If the dog is kept indoors, it's a good idea to regularly brush her coat, not only to keep the animal looking good, but also to keep oil in her hair and remove dead hair. Grooming will also enable you to see any skin problems, injuries, or insects such as fleas or ticks, so that you can deal with them sooner rather than later.

How you groom your dog depends on the length of the dog's hair. If you have a short haired breed, the best tool for grooming is a stiff brush and a chamois cloth. First, brush the dog's hair several times in the direction it grows. When you are finished with the brush, rub the chamois cloth over the coat to shine it up a little. The entire procedure need last no longer than 15 minutes.

If the dog has a medium coat, say of the density of one found on the Chesapeake Bay Retriever, you should use a brush-like tool called a slicker brush. This is a brush with bent metal bristles. Just run this

Regular brushing will keep shedding to a minimum.

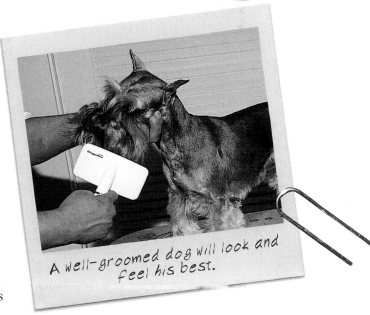

A well-groomed dog will look and feel his best.

Part 2

Dogs that compete in shows need special grooming.

Finding a Good Groomer

If you think that finding a good grooomer is really simple, you're wrong. There are good ones and not-so-good ones, and it's worth the search to get a good one.

Ask your vet, friends who have dogs, and your breeder who they recommend. Then have a conversation with the groomer. You should tell the groomer that you will deliver the dog at a certain hour and want to know exactly when you'll get him back—no open-ended hours. Normally, unless the coat is horrendously matted, a wash and clip shouldn't take more than two to four hours.

Because your pooch is going into a place where other dogs visit, make sure she has all her vaccinations, most particularly against kennel cough. Make sure that you and the groomer are on the same page (unlike the groomer who did my dog Misty) as far as the finished result is concerned.

One final tip: If you're getting your dog groomed to pretty her up for Christmas, make an appointment months in advance. It's the most popular time to have dogs groomed.

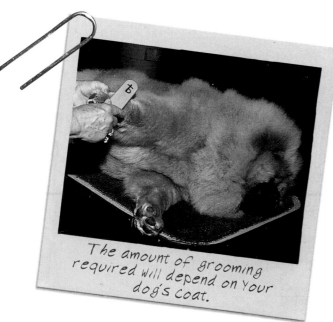

The amount of grooming required will depend on your dog's coat.

over a dog as you would a regular brush. It will do a good job removing dead hair and energizing the skin. Follow this with a regular brushing and finish with a chamois.

For dogs with long hair that can mat, such as Afghan Hounds, the best procedure is to start off with a pin brush, which is one that has straight bristles, and a comb once all mats have been cleared (something, but the way, that will be lessened with frequent grooming). It's best to start grooming from the bottom of the legs up, so that you can be sure that the entire coat, not just the top layer of hair, is completely clear of mats.

If you have a dog that needs a lot of grooming or has a hard-to-maintain coat, you may decide to get a groomer. People usually get one for spaniels, terriers, and double-coated dogs like Shetland Sheepdogs and Collies. Your breeder should be able to recommend a groomer in your area.

Nail Care

The nails on your dog's paws are sanded off naturally as they walk along hard surfaces, but if your dog mostly walks on grass or carpet, the terrain is too soft to do the job. Long nails can hook into the carpet and injure the dog's foot, leading to lameness.

How can you tell if your dog's nails are too long? The nails should have a blunt appearance and be even with the bottom of the paws, and her paws should not make clicking sounds when she walks on the flooring.

An inexpensive nail clipper can be used to trim your dog's nails. If you are inexperienced, take only a short potion of each nail off. You want to avoid cutting into the vein that runs down the nail. If you cut the bottom portion of the nail (the quick) too short, it will bleed. If this happens, dab it with styptic pencil.

Dental Care

If you take care of your dog's teeth, you shouldn't have any problems when she reaches old age. However, if she is fed a steady diet of soft foot, tartar builds up and leads to decay. The best way to avoid this is to keep your dog

If you don't want to spend time grooming your dog, hire a professional.

Keep your dog's nails trimmed to prevent injuries.

Part 2

Good oral hygiene is essential to your dog's health.

Your dog's teeth should be white and his breath fresh.

on a hard food diet and occasionally feed her some hard biscuits or a chewable Nylabone™.

If tartar builds up, either you or your vet can remove it. You can brush your dog's teeth using a canine toothbrush and cleanser.

Key Points

• Learn the symptoms of dangerous diseases.

• Puppy-proof your home by looking at a room's from puppy's point of view and removing anything that might be dangerous.

• Become familiar with substances that are hazardous to a dog.

• Put the Poison Control Center number in prominent place.

• Have a first aid kit handy.

• Groom your dog on a regular basis.

Part Three
Basic Training

"Ok then, we'll compromise. Half the treat now, and half the treat AFTER I sit."

Housetraining and Puppy Training

It is very difficult, perhaps impossible, to name anything cuter than a puppy. However, the puppy's cuteness is his secret weapon when it comes to training. He's just so cute that you shy away from giving him any corrections–such as an authoritative, "No!"–in fear that it might upset him. The fact is, however, that in order to train a puppy to do and not do certain things, he must know when he is pleasing or displeasing you.

It's a good idea to get the puppy into your own personal kindergarten so that he can learn the household rules sooner rather than later. These rules will make your life, as well as his, much easier and more pleasant.

What your puppy wants most is to please you.

Start training your puppy as early as possible.

Part 3

There's another important reason to start training your puppy early: A dog's training schedule is related; early training procedures get his little paws wet and introduce him to training, and some training procedures can only be accomplished if others have proceeded them. As trainer Linda Rudolph says, "You can't train a dog to give you its paw if it has not first been trained to sit."

The kindergarten course should consist of housetraining, curbing the dog's chewing, and stopping inappropriate behaviors.

Housetraining

One of the most important things a puppy must learn is to do his business in a place where it is not objectionable. If he doesn't become housetrained, he can never learn to live as part of your family.

Before you start, the puppy should have all his shots to protect him from disease. Most experts say housetraining should start when a puppy is eight weeks or older, and one can expect, depending on variables such as the type of dog, that the procedure will take anywhere from three days to three weeks.

If you live in a house that has easy access to the great outdoors, there are a couple of ways to housetrain your puppy. Living in an apartment presents special problems, but housetraining can be done.

As with any training procedure, the keys are to be consistent, be firm, and let the puppy know when he's doing the right or wrong thing, right away. Timing is key. If

No!

I believe that the word "No" is one of the most important words you can utter in training exercises, whether it is housetraining or other training. As soon as you can, it's a good idea to teach the puppy that this word means that he is not to continue a particular behavior.

Your first task is to get the puppy to understand what this word means; i.e., that the puppy is doing something that does not please you.

After a while—and it may take more than a while—he'll get the idea. Then when he does things he shouldn't do, you'll have a verbal tool to stop him.

What's in a Name?

Never use your puppy's name in a negative way, especially when correcting him. If you do, he may start to associate his name with punishment, and he will not respond to it positively. This is especially important later in training, when you are teaching him basic obedience commands, such as coming when called.

you don't correct him in a timely way, the puppy won't understand and won't be able to connect his act with your correction. I remember a friend of mine discovered that his Beagle puppy had used his inlaid kitchen floor as a bathroom without benefit of paper. My friend, who had had a tough day at the office, started to harangue the dog, and the Beagle promptly beat a hasty retreat. He then looked up at my friend with one of the most adorable looks I have ever seen in my life.

I said, "Hey, Joe, do you think his puppy mind can comprehend what you're saying?"

Joe's adult mind comprehended what I was saying, and soon we were both laughing. Joe gave the puppy a hug, which he understood really well.

Your dog will not understand if you correct him for something he did hours or even minutes before. You must catch him in the act for the correction to work. This is why it is important to watch your dog very carefully when housetraining him. If the puppy seems like he has to go out (if he is scratching, circling, sniffing, or squatting) say, "No!" firmly and immediately get him outside. Then praise

Timing and praise are the keys to training your puppy.

Positive reinforcement is a big part of the training process.

him for going outside. If you come home to a mess, simply clean it up and wait for an opportunity to show the puppy the correct behavior.

Outside Time

Perhaps the least complicated way to housetrain a puppy is to take him outside to do his business. Puppies need to go a lot–they are babies, after all, with small bladders and little ability to control themselves–and you want to take them outside frequently.

When he's inside, you want to confine the puppy to a place where his instincts will deter him from going. To do this, confine him to a small area, such as a wire crate or a pen, or to a section of the kitchen or bathroom (which has a non-absorbent floor in case of accidents) that you've segmented off with a board or baby fence. This will also serve as his temporary home within your home. He will try to avoid eliminating in his space and fouling where he lives, so he will start holding himself in check more and more as he matures. (Don't put him in a basement or garage, because this isolates him from his pack and will make him lonely and miserable.)

Confining your puppy to a crate may seem like a cruel and inhumane thing to do, but it isn't. A puppy will get used to it and even come to regard it as his own special place. Many dog owners, for example, will keep a crate after housetraining is over but leave the door open so the dog can go back and forth inside it. This allows the dog to have his own place where he can retreat, away from the human world.

The easiest way to housetrain your puppy is to teach him to eliminate outside.

When housetraining, confine your puppy to a small area while indoors.

Part 3

If you use this method of confinement, housetraining your dog will be accomplished very rapidly. Far from being inhumane, it will ensure that you and the dog can live together in harmony for years to come.

Routine

Routine is important. You should take the dog out after every meal and as often as you're able to in between meals. Also take him out when you first wake up in the morning; you will probably feel the urge to go and so will he.

Avoid giving him water at least two hours before you take him out for the last time of the day. You should also take him out as late as night as possible, so he has a better chance of lasting the whole night without an accident.

All told, half a dozen to eight outside times per day should be sufficient. A sample schedule might be:

6:30 am: Walk

7:00 am: Feed and walk

11:00 am: Feed and walk

4:00 pm: Feed and walk

7:00 pm: Last water of day and walk

10:30 pm: Walk

Praise

As with other training procedures, praise is very important. When your puppy does his business outside, make a big deal of it (and it is a big deal when he's not going in the

A regular outside schedule will speed up the housetraining process.

Part 3

Successful training depends on both the dog and the owner.

Praise your puppy when he eliminates outside.

house). Praise him lavishly, look into his eyes, and tell him how pleased you are with him.

It's important to be sincere–a dog can tell if you're giving him baloney–and let your tone of voice show that you're happy. Dogs want to please their human alphas. If he knows that eliminating outside pleases you, he will make an effort to do it again.

If you catch him going inside the house, by all means correct him. As mentioned earlier, startle him in to stopping him while you bark, "No! No! No! No!" so that he'll know that what he is doing is not acceptable. Assuming he stops, grab the leash and get him outside immediately so he can connect your disapproval with his voiding.

We are all human, and at times you may lose your temper and be tempted to push the puppy's face into his waste. This is cruel, and it won't teach the dog anything except to fear you. Of course, never hit the dog. He won't connect being hit with his accident, and it will only make him more difficult to deal with.

Once he's done his business, he can be played with and otherwise nurtured and socialized–he needn't stay in his own place all the time. He has not been sentenced to solitary crate confinement or, for that matter, any kind of jail. Housetraining actually gives your puppy the freedom to become a part of the family.

Paper Training
Some people use a paper training method to housetrain their dog, which gradually and literally leads to the dog going outside. This usually works

Praise, Praise, Praise!

When puppies are very young, they will not understand the words you use. "Good dog" will mean nothing to him until he later begins to associate the words with his actions. Always use a happy tone of voice when praising your puppy—the voice tone will be more meaningful to him than the actual words. Also, when beginning training, verbal praise should be combined with petting for a few months in his young life before a puppy will understand verbal praise alone.

well for people that live in apartments or do not have easy access to the outdoors. For this method to work, first spread newspaper or pads that you can buy in a pet store over the floor of a room such as the kitchen or bath–somewhere with a non-absorbent surface beneath. Then, when the puppy voids, it will associate the paper or pads, which he feels through his paws, with voiding.

Once he gets used to this (it usually takes a few days), you can gradually reduce the amount of paper or pads in the room so that when he wants to go, he has to search for the paper. As you reduce the paper or pads, move them toward a door that leads outside.

Paper training is one way to housetrain your dog.

At one point, put the paper outside with just a corner of it under the door for the puppy to see. When you see the puppy is interested in the paper, open the door so he can go outside, walk on it, and void. Naturally, every time he voids on the paper, laud his efforts sincerely. Conversely, if he doesn't use the paper, let him know that you disapprove by saying, "No!"

Once outside, place the pad in the spot where you want the puppy to go all the time and then gradually make the area smaller and smaller. The idea is for him to be more focused on the

This Labrador Retriever gets a reward for a job well done.

Part 3

Take your puppy to the same spot every time to eliminate.

place than the pad, and once this happens, the pad can be withdrawn completely.

As you can see–particularly if you live in an apartment–housetraining a dog can require considerable effort, especially with certain breeds that don't take to it too well. Not only must you be ever alert to impending disaster, but it also takes willpower and energy to extricate yourself from that warm couch at the end of the night or out of your cozy bed early in the morning to take the puppy out, particularly if the weather is nasty. However, the effort you put into housetraining in the beginning will be well worth it, because you are building the training blocks of trust and discipline with your dog.

Feeding

For all their toughness, resilience, and wolf lineage, dogs have sensitive stomachs. In order to housetrain a puppy properly, the food he ingests during training must help to keep that stomach quiescent. If it isn't, it can result in loose stools, diarrhea, or urinating excessively, problems that can defeat the housetraining process before it starts.

Give the puppy a brand of food that will enhance his chances of having normal bowel movements. Do not switch the puppy's food suddenly, as this is sure to result in stomach upset. Feed a young puppy the same brand of food that he had been eating from his previous home. If you wish to change brands, do so gradually, mixing the new food with the old until the puppy's stomach is settled. It is suggested that you feed your dog one part canned dog food to three parts moistened dry dog food. It's important, again, to follow routine: Feed, walk, and water the dog at the same times every day.

A puppy must get all the food he needs to meet his nutritional needs; however, if you find that he's leaving food in his bowl, it means that he's getting too much, so you should feed him less. If he's going to the bathroom excessively, it may mean the same thing.

As mentioned, a dog's stomach is sensitive, so you should not feed him table scraps during his training period or violate the schedule in any way. Of course, you shouldn't leave food and water on the floor all day. The more he eats and drinks, the greater the likelihood of him going to the bathroom when he shouldn't.

Accidents

Despite your most diligent efforts, puppies will have accidents. When you clean up after him, first put the dog out of the way; you don't want the puppy to get the idea that this is your regular job (as it was the mother's when the puppy was very young).

If the puppy goes on a non-absorbent surface, such as linoleum or tile, cleanup won't be a problem. Just wipe it up with a rag and floor cleanser. If the puppy goes on your carpet, it's more problematic. The idea is to get it up as quickly as possible, picking any stools up and blotting the wetness with paper towel.

There are a variety of products for cleaning up and killing odors available at your local pet store or supermarket. You can also neutralize the urine with plain white vinegar or sprinkle baking soda over the spot and sweep it up when dry. A diarrhea stain can be handled with commercial products as well as a solution

Offer your dog food and water at the same times every day.

Papers on the floor will make cleaning up accidents easier.

Part 3

of lukewarm water, dishwashing soap, and vinegar. (Incidentally, never mix products containing bleach and ammonia: toxic fumes are created.)

However, it should be remembered that merely cleaning up the stain is not good enough to prevent the dog from going again in the same spot. Dogs have fantastic olfactory skills and can detect smells that the human nose wouldn't have a chance of smelling. If they can smell where they have gone before, then that's exactly where they'll go again: "marking" their urine or defecation what is known as a "scent post." In so many words, if the spot where the dog is still accessible the dog's sense of smell, then housetraining will not occur.

None of the standard household products, such as vinegar, ammonia, or bleach, will keep the dog from finding the same spot. The only thing available is an odor neutralizer concentrate that is available at pet stores and pharmacies.

Before removing any kind of a stain from carpeting or sensitive flooring, test the remover in an out-of-the-way spot (such as under a couch) to make sure that it doesn't damage the color.

If your floors are wood and protected by polyurethane, cleaning up an accident shouldn't be a problem. But if the polyurethane is worn down and raw wood exposed or the floors are unprotected, the urine can seep down into the fibers of the wood, ultimately turning them black. Removing this kind of stain cannot be done easily, and you may have to cut out the damaged boards and replace them.

Puppy Problems

Like babies, puppies are subject to having a variety of behavior problems. However, when caught early enough, the problem behavior can be curbed.

Chewing

Part of a puppy's natural instinct is to chew, and his little teeth are good for the purpose. While he doesn't have a strong bite, his teeth are brand new and very sharp, and they can do a horrific amount of damage. If you go away during the day and allow the puppy free rein of the house, he may demonstrate this to you by chewing on couch legs, kitchen cabinets, carpet, drapes–whatever his mouth can reach. He also can chew on electrical wires, which, of course, is dangerous.

There are a couple of ways to stop a puppy from chewing on your belongings. One way is to simply house the puppy in his carrier, crate, or other separated area. To determine what can be a problem, get down on your hands and knees and take a puppy's-eye-view of things. Remove what ever might be a target, and if you can't (say a telephone wire is stapled to a baseboard), spray it with one of the bitter-tasting products that will make it unpalatable to the pup.

Another way to stop your puppy from chewing on your belongings is to provide him with bones and toys that he can chew on safely. Nylabone™ makes many products that are great for teething puppies, and you can also provide him with treats to keep his teeth occupied and off your furniture.

Biting

Puppies explore with their mouths, and often bite or nip by accident when playing. This most often happens when children are involved, because when it comes to knowing the right thing to do, little kids are more or less like puppies. They will grab a puppy by the tail, poke a finger in an eye, or otherwise manhandle the dog, all in the name of play. Unfortunately, playtime can get out of control, or the puppy may have a bad reaction and nip the kid.

To prevent this from happening, children should be instructed on how to handle a puppy gently, and the two should never be left to play unsupervised. If the puppy does nip, he should be given a firm, "No!" and the two should be separated for a time-out. Kids and

With the proper training, any puppy can become a good canine citizen.

Toys give your dog a safe chewing alternative.

Part 3

Children should be taught to handle puppies gently.

dogs can grow up to be the best of friends if they learn from the very beginning to respect one another.

Crying at Night

It's important to understand why puppies cry like this: Essentially, the puppy perceives that he has been separated from his pack, and the whining and crying is an attempt to identify where the pack is and return to it.

One way to solve the problem is to remember that you are now part of the pack and move the crate or carrier into your bedroom. The puppy, hopefully, will be back with his pack and will quiet down.

Sometimes this doesn't work. If you have moved the crate into your bedroom and the puppy keeps on whining, then tap your hand on the crate and say "No-sleep!" or "No-quiet!"

If this still doesn't work, give him a little chew toy to play with. Above all, don't implicitly approve of the whining by comforting him and letting him sleep with you–it's an easy trap to fall into. None of us wants to be alone (most of the time). Be firm, but don't yell or frighten the puppy; this just makes things worse. Comfort him with your voice and your presence, and in time, he'll get used to his new surroundings.

It's also a good idea to play vigorously with the puppy before he goes to sleep. A very tired puppy will sleep, not whine.

Key Points

• Start the puppy's housetraining early–as soon as he comes home with you.

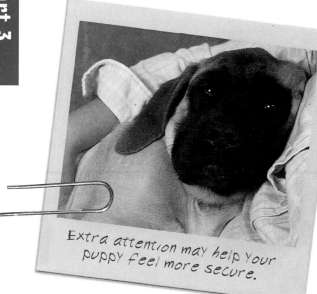

Extra attention may help your puppy feel more secure.

• Confine the puppy as part of your housetraining procedure and when you cannot supervise him.

• Your dog will not understand the correction if you correct him for something he did hours or even minutes before. You must catch him in the act for the correction to work.

• If you come home to a mess, simply clean it up and wait for an opportunity to show the puppy the correct behavior.

• When the pup does something right, praise him lavishly.

• Establish a routine to take the dog outside to eliminate.

• Be sincere when speaking with the dog. Watch your tone of voice and body language.

• If the dog has an accident in the house, use a special product to remove it. Otherwise, the dog will seek out the same spot.

Mysterious Behaviors

Puppies exhibit a variety of behaviors that may at first mystify or concern you, but are perfectly normal. For example:

• A puppy may fall asleep while doing something else. Puppies do need a lot of sleep, but because they have a very short attention span, they may forget to sleep. Their bodies will suddenly realize this while they're eating, playing with a toy, or even running.

• A puppy may twitch while sleeping. This just indicates that his nervous system is developing normally. It will be most common during the first few months of a puppy's life, and then slowly diminish, though some adult dogs will continue to twitch.

Part 3

• In order to prevent kids from being nipped, teach them how to be gentle with the new puppy and always supervise their playtime together.

• Give the puppy a firm "No!" when he misbehaves, but don't get angry–he has to know where he stands.

Obedience Commands

After housetraining, obedience training is crucial if you expect to be able to control your dog at home, in the neighborhood, and in special situations where her training could save her life.

There are six basic commands that every dog should know: heel, sit, stay, stand-stay, down, and come. The dog must not only respond to them, but she should respond to them in one command.

Conditioning

Your dog is able to learn these commands because of the underlying principle of conditioning. You dog should be conditioned to perform each command: A stimulus is applied and the dog is

Obedience training is necessary in order to control your dog.

Dog Days

When one speaks of the "dog days," it means that things are moving more slowly than usual and are not as good as they could be.

As it happens, dogs should not be connected to the phrase at all. According to Desmond Morris in his book *Dog Watching*, it seems to have originated during the Roman times, when Romans thought that the dog star Sirius would add its heat to that of the sun during the hottest parts of the summer, July 3 to August 1.

This, of course, is not true, but Sirius is in fact twice as hot as the sun, which is about 5,000 degrees. But as hot as it is, it's not really a problem, because it's 540,000 times as far from us as the sun!

A chain-link collar is a useful piece of training equipment.

conditioned to respond a certain way.

The classic example of conditioning was Pavlov's experiments with dogs. He conditioned the dogs to expect food every time he rang a bell. They got to a point where they would salivate in anticipation of food when the bell rang, even though none was forthcoming.

Conditioning is accomplished by repetition; i.e., repeating the exercise over and over again until it becomes second nature. The dog is conditioned, with guidance from the trainer, to what is right behavior and what is wrong. When the dog does something right, she gets praise from her owner, issued in a soft, gentle, but honest and enthusiastic way: "Good dog!" When she does something wrong, she is told, firmly, "No!" Dogs don't like disapproval, because they seek to please their owners.

Supplies

Before you start training your dog, you should have at your disposal a training collar, sometimes called a "choke" or "slip" collar, which won't choke her at all if you use it properly.

The collar is a length of chain with a ring on each end. One ringed end is slipped through the other ringed end, and then a leash or lead is snapped onto the ring that was slipped through. When you pull on it gently, it tightens around the dog's neck and acts as a corrective tool. When you let up the pressure, the collar relaxes. To get the right size collar, measure the distance around the largest part of the dog's head and then add one inch. It's important to put the collar on correctly to avoid choking the dog and to have it work as it should. The best bet is to ask the proprietor of the pet store how to do it.

You should also have a lead or leash. It may be made of leather or webbing and should be a half-inch to one-inch wide and six feet long. The first thing to do is to put on the training collar, clip on the leash, and let the puppy get used to dragging it around. When working with a leash, always leave some slack in it, so the dog doesn't feel any tension, and she gets used to the idea of walking with one on.

Commands

Training commands must be consistent, no matter who is in charge of the dog's care. If they are not, the dog will get mixed messages, and the training will fail.

The Heel Command

When a dog heels, it means that she walks beside you on your left side, neither pulling ahead or lagging behind, nor that you have her under control.

First, with your dog wearing her collar and leash, take a step, starting with your left foot, and at the same time, call out the name of the dog, "Spot, heel!" Give her a gentle tug with the leash to get her moving.

A retractable leash will aid in the training process.

Make sure you have your dog's full attention before teaching him a command.

The heel command makes your daily walks more enjoyable.

Training sessions should be short and end on a positive note.

As you walk, strive to get the dog walking so her head and shoulder are aligned with the front of your left leg and to keep it in alignment by issuing those gentle tugs and repeated commands: "Spot, heel!"

Every time you give a tug and a command and the dog responds, give her praise, "Good girl!" Praise is essential because even though the tugs may be mild, they still cause the dog discomfort. You want to clearly demonstrate that this is not your purpose, that you still love her, and that you are pleased with her actions. The praise does all that.

In fact, the training collar is your key aid to get your dog to heel on command. However, don't overdo it—a quick tug and release should be enough for her to get the message.

As with all training, sessions should not be too long. Lengthy training sessions can result in a loss of concentration and boredom, making it very difficult to end on a positive note. In the beginning, exercises that are done twice a day for 15 minutes each are fine. When your dog is obeying reliably, you can then gradually increase training exercises to 30 minutes.

Your goal is get the dog to heel without having to tug on the leash. Another goal, as in all training, is to have the dog obey with a single command. If she doesn't, she's not trained properly.

Your Left Foot

Using your left foot is not happenstance. You should start with it whenever you issue a command; the puppy will associate the movement of the left foot with training. On the other hand (or foot!), if you want the dog to remain stationary, it's a good idea to start with your right foot as you walk away from the dog.

Once the dog gets the idea, don't just walk in a straight line. Do figure eights, curves, and circles. Snap the leash and praise as needed until you know that the dog is following you on her own.

The dog might have some difficulty. After all, she's going through her first real training procedure, but stay with it. The heel command comes in handy in any number of situations, such as when you're walking through a crowd or when there are other pooches present.

The Sit Command

The sit command should result in your dog sitting on her rump immediately to the left of the handler, her shoulder aligned with the handler's knee. The dog should assume the sit position when she stops moving or heeling.

Say the command, "Sit!" as the dog is heeling next to you, and at the same time, use your left hand to gently push her rump down while your right hand tugs the leash upward, lifting her head. Praise her when she sits, and then give her the heel command and start walking. Repeat the sit command and procedure, but this time, let her stay seated a little longer. Don't forget the praise.

Keep repeating the procedure, and after a while, the dog will automatically stop and sit when you stop—no command or tug of the lead will be required. Eventually, she will be ready to move again, only when you move or release her from the sit.

Your dog must be able to perform basic commands if he is to compete in dog shows.

The sit command is the foundation for all other commands.

Part 3

This Bloodhound gets a little help learning how to sit.

If your dog has trouble understanding a command, show him what to do.

Once she's grasped the sit command, the next step is to teach her to sit without heeling. Put the collar and leash on her and tell her to sit. If she doesn't yet associate the word with the action, you can use a treat or a toy. Simply raise the treat above the dog's head and tell her to "Sit!" She should sit automatically, and she can receive the treat along with praise.

The Stay Command

To introduce the stay command, start with the dog heeling on her lead and then stop. The dog should sit and then, this time starting with your right foot, take a step away and say, "Stay!" Also, put your left hand in front of her muzzle, with your palm facing her nose. If you have to, hold her stationary with your hand—you want to make sure that she stays and that she connects what she's doing with the command.

Repeat the procedure, moving away from her a little further each time she stays in place. Have patience; this especially hard for young dogs that just want to follow their owners. Start with only a few seconds at a time, gradually increasing the time

Will Work for Food

Teach your dog to work for a living—all dogs love to think that they have a purpose, and performing basic commands allows them to receive your praise. Make your pup sit before she gets her meals or a treat or have her sit before you take her outside. Have your dog stay while you're on the telephone or before you throw the ball for her to fetch. When you use basic commands in everyday situations, you are reinforcing your dog's training on a daily basis.

you require her to stay as she matures and begins to understand the command. If necessary, use your hands to restrain her, not in a cruel way but just to demonstrate what the stay command means.

The Stand-Stay Command

Once the dog has learned to sit and stay, you can teach her to stand and stay. This can be a very valuable command in a variety of situations, such as when the dog must stand up straight when being examined by a vet or while being groomed. The stand command is also important if you wish to compete in conformation shows with your dog, as she must stand still to be inspected by the judges.

Start the dog heeling on her leash and then come to a halt. Before she can sit, put your hand, fingers spread, in front of her right hind leg, stopping her from going into the sit position and simultaneously telling her to "Stand-Stay."

She may try to sit–why wouldn't she? As you work, keep the praise coming as she stands. Before she can sit, start heeling again and repeat the procedure. Occasionally let her sit when you stop, and when you want her to stand, say the word and block her going into the sitting position.

Soon the idea will imprint itself: She is to sit automatically when she stops heeling, but she is to stand and stay when she hears the command. At one point, all you'll have to do is utter, "Stand," and she'll stand and stay. Once you have the dog standing and staying or sitting and staying, you can start moving away from her, and when you do, she will hold his position.

Use hand signals with verbal commands.

The stand-stay command is useful in many situations.

Part 3

This dog stands for an examination by a conformation judge.

Start with the command, "Stay!" and reinforce it by holding your left hand in front of her muzzle.

Then, take a step away and start to move away from her. If she breaks position, tell her, "No!" and "Stay!" Have patience, because prior to this, the dog was trained to heel when the handler started to move. Practice the command again until she knows she is to stay until you tell her to heel.

Once she gets the idea of staying while you move away, repeat the command and make the dog hold the position for longer and longer periods of time, until she can hold the stand position for a minute or so.

Again, just continue to practice until you can circle around her a few times and she stays or stands—and don't forget the praise.

The Down Command

To teach the down command, start by kneeling beside the dog while she is sitting. Reach over with your left hand so that you can grab her left front leg and use your right hand to lift her paws and gently lower her to the ground, saying, "Down."

Be sure to associate the down command with positive rewards.

Once down, tell her, "Down-Stay," keeping your left hand on her back. Keep her this way for a few seconds, then command her to sit and praise her. If you keep repeating the procedure, you'll eventually get to the point where she will go down on the command alone. After plenty of practice, you should also be able to walk away from her while she remains in position.

The Come Command

This is perhaps the most important command because it enables you to get your dog out of harm's way with one word, "Come!"

Start by heeling with the dog, then take an abrupt step backward, tugging the leash to make the dog turn right, and say, "Come!" Continue to walk backward with the dog following you, aided by gentle tugs on the leash and the repetition of the come command.

Keep up a steady stream of praise. Eventually, you should be able to just step back, say, "Come," and the dog should come toward you and then sit down. Once she's sitting, step back to the full length of the lead and tell her to come again. Repeat this procedure. Gradually, you will be able to advance to the point where you can use a retractable leash. You can put the dog in a stay position, then retreat back 25 or 30 feet and call the dog toward you.

It Takes Time

Training a dog takes time and patience. One dog might be able to learn all the commands in a few weeks, while another dog might take three or four months, even if they are members of the same breed. Many people find it great fun to train a dog, particularly when positive results start to emerge, and once the dog learns, she won't forget.

Key Points

• Teaching your dog basic commands can save her life and make your lives together much easier.

Your dog may need encouragement to get into the down position.

The down command may be hard for more dominant dogs to master.

Part 3

The come command may save your dog's life some day.

If You Want Help

If you want to get some professional assistance in training your dog, it is available.

You can go to a dog trainer or enroll in a class offered by a park or recreation group in your area. Humane societies and shelters offer other programs for owners who adopt their dogs. Other good sources are the AKC, your breeder (if you have one), a veterinarian, or friends or associates who have had dogs trained.

• Key aids in training a dog are a training or "choke" collar and a six-foot leash.

• An important element in dog training is repetition of commands.

• When a puppy does something right, she should be lavishly praised.

• Training takes a while. Don't get discouraged.

Use a happy tone of voice when you call your dog to you.

Canine Good Citizen® Test

Dogs have an image, and it seems safe to say that it is a good image in general. Dogs are viewed as loving, loyal, and cute–a fantastic pet. They generally are. Unfortunately, not all dogs are well behaved. Some are viewed as rude, crude, and just plain dangerous, which some happen to be. The reasons why good dogs go bad vary, but in most cases, it is the fault of the owners. Bad dogs rarely come out of good owners.

The American Kennel Club is concerned with the image of dogs everywhere, and in order to improve the image of the dog, they have instituted the Canine Good Citizen® Award. This award, which is granted when a dog passes the Canine Good Citizen® Test, is conducted by clubs affiliated with the AKC, as well

A canine good citizen is an asset to the community.

Every dog can benefit from basic training.

Contacting the AKC

To contact the AKC about the
Canine Good Citizen® Test:

American Kennel Club
5580 Centerview Avenue
Raleigh, NC 27606
919-233-9767
www.akc.org

as other organizations, such as the Delta Society and Therapy Dogs International. It was first instituted on September 1, 1989.

Before the Test

Following the information in this book will likely enable your dog to pass the Canine Good Citizen® Test. However, there are some additional things you should do to increase your chances.

If you are the dog's handler, it's important that you are relaxed during the test–the dog will sense if you're not and that could affect his performance. To help ensure this, you should practice the test with your dog before actually taking it. Before the test, let the dog run around as a warm up. Your dog should be groomed and bathed before the test. Also, make sure your dog has gone to the bathroom long enough before the test so that he doesn't go during it.

The test is actually composed of ten different tests, and both purebred dogs and mixed breeds

Good manners allow your dog to accompany you anywhere.

Part 3

are eligible to take it. If the dog passes, he is issued a certificate testifying to his achievement–and it is an achievement. While the dog doesn't have to be St. Francis of Assisi to pass, those who do are certainly more saint than sinner.

The ten parts of the test are conducted at ten different stations by different examiners. Basically, dogs that pass the test look good and act well. If you follow the information contained in previous chapters on appearance and training and have taught your dog good behavior, your pooch should have no trouble passing, although as suggested earlier, you should thoroughly familiarize yourself with the test and practice before you take it. Practice, as they say, makes perfect.

A well-groomed dog is a pleasure to be around.

The following are the parts of the test and some tips to help improve your dog's chances of passing.

Appearance and Grooming

The purpose of this portion of the test is not only to determine that the dog looks good and is healthy, but that that he will permit others to groom and examine him. Many professional groomers can tell you nasty stories about animals that were not so inclined and made their jobs unpleasant or downright hazardous.

The examiner will not only check the dog's appearance, but will also do a hands-on exercise, picking up each of the front feet and lightly combing the dog (the owner must supply the brush and/or comb he regularly uses) to see how the pooch reacts. He is allowed to move around as he wishes and doesn't have to hold a specific position.

The stay command is useful when grooming your dog.

Your dog should accept anyone that you accept, including children.

He must not, of course, be antsy or hostile, and the owner is allowed to encourage the dog during the test.

The examiner will also take note of the dog's appearance as it relates to health. If the dog has runny eyes, dry skin, or any of a number of other maladies, these should be addressed before the dog is tested.

Accepting a Stranger

This part of the test measures how accepting the dog is of friendly strangers. The owner will be instructed to have the dog stand next to him. The examiner will approach, greeting the owner without apparently paying any attention to the dog, and see how the dog reacts. He should not react with shyness or aggression. Here's a tip: If the dog starts this part of the test in a sitting position, which is allowed, he is less likely to move while the examiner and owner talk. If the dog moves during the conversation between the owner and examiner, it's a reason to fail the dog.

Why Do Dogs Pant?

A well-known dog trainer I know once said: "It has nothing to do with him falling in love."

Rather, it has to do with cooling the body. As dogs developed throughout the ages, a thick, furry coat was necessary to protect them against the frigid winters. They also needed an outlet for their sweating, particularly in summer, so they developed paws that they sweat through.

This is fine, except paws are relatively small parts of a dog's body, and they needed a way to cool their bodies down more rapidly. This resulted in panting. Dogs open their mouths, exposing their tongues to the heated air coming out of their bodies, and it cools it—and them—by evaporation. To hasten the process they also consume large amounts of water.

It doesn't matter how much or little hair a dog has; they all sweat through their paws. Even the Mexican hairless dog sweats through his paws, even though his coat looks like skin. Indeed, Desmond Morris points out in his book, *Dogwatching*, that it is believed that the Mexicans developed the dogs as "human hot water bottles."

Walk on Loose Lead

This test is designed to demonstrate that the handler can control the dog. As in all obedience competition, the dog must be walked to the left of the examiner. As the dog is walked by, the examiner will ask the handler to make the dog turn left, right, and around, as well as stop and halt. During the walk, the dog does not have to be in the standard "heel" position (but, as mentioned, he will be to the left of the handler), and the handler may talk to the dog, praising him as needed.

The use of the leash will be very carefully observed: Guiding with a tight lead or a quick jerk can result in disqualification. In other words, the dog will be graded on what he does naturally, not what he is forced to do.

Your dog should be able to walk nicely beside you on his leash.

Walk Through a Crowd

In this test, the dog must walk through a crowd without yielding to the distractions created by the examiners. The dog must go by a variety of people–at least three–that are moving around in some way; for example, one may be sweeping and another may be bouncing a ball. As in other aspects of the test, the handler is allowed to encourage the dog. If he yields to the distraction by jumping at the person or otherwise losing his concentration, he can fail.

Sit Politely for Petting

The dog, on a leash, should be sitting next to his owner on either side. The examiner will then approach the dog from the front and pet him on the

Socialization ensures that your dog will enjoy the company of people.

The examiner should be able to pet your dog on the head and body.

head and body only. Once this is completed, the examiner will circle the dog. The dog must allow the examiner to pet and circle him without any negative reactions.

Sit, Down, and Stay Commands

This test demonstrates that the dog has had basic training and will obey his handler's commands. The handler will be required to make the dog sit and then go down. The handler will be allowed a reasonable amount of time to complete these commands and is also allowed to touch the dog to encourage him. However, pushing the dog's rump down into position will disqualify the dog immediately.

The next part of the test determines if the dog will stay in the position when he is told. The dog is connected to a 20-foot line. The handler must first command the dog to sit or go down, walk away from the dog without dropping the leash, and then walk back toward the dog without him changing his position.

Come Command

This test determines if the dog will come to his handler on command. Leaving the dog in the stay or down position, the handler unleashes the dog and then walks away ten feet. Next, he turns back toward the dog and calls for him to come. The dog should keep his stationary position until told to come, but the examiner may help by distracting the dog by petting him or doing something else until the handler calls him.

Reacting to Other Dogs

This test will determine how well a dog will get

The handler must be able to command the dog to sit, go down, and stay.

Part 3

along with other dogs. The test starts with two handlers facing each other from a distance of ten yards, each with a dog on their left sides.

They walk toward one another, greet each other, and walk by about five yards, during which the tested dog should not make any attempt to get to the other dog, either to socialize or to be aggressive.

Your puppy should come to you on command.

Distractions

This is the ultimate distraction test because the distractions come as a total surprise to the dog. The examiner picks any two distractions, and the dog may react with slight alarm or concern but should not bark madly, run away, or show aggressiveness. The handler can praise the dog during the exercise. The distractions can be any of the following:

√ A person in a wheelchair or on crutches;

√ A door suddenly opening or closing;

√ A large book dropping no further than ten feet behind the dog;

√ A jogger running in front of the dog;

Getting along with other dogs is part of the Canine Good Citizen test.

A CGC title means that your dog is a productive member of society.

Your dog should feel comfortable being left with another person.

√ People near the dog interacting with one another in a playful, animated way;

√ A person pushing a cart pauses within ten feet of the dog;

√ A person rides a bicycle approaching from the front or rear of the dog and within six feet;

√ A chair is knocked over no closer than six feet from the dog.

Supervised Separation

This part of the test shows that a dog can be left with a stranger without the dog exhibiting anything but mild annoyance. Using a six-foot leash, the owner should hand the dog over to the examiner and go away for three minutes. The dog may move around, but he should not exhibit anything but mild annoyance at his handler's absence.

A Series of Questions

In addition to the specific tests, the examiner asks himself a series of questions about the dog as the tests proceed:

√ Is this the kind of dog I would like to own?

√ Is it safe to have children around this dog?

√ Would I welcome this dog if it became a neighbor of mine?

√ Is this dog making his owner happy as well as not making someone else unhappy?

Key Points

• Passing the Canine Good Citizen® Test means that your dog is a well-behaved member of society and will be a great pet to his family and neighbor to the community.

• If your dog can learn the training exercises in this book, he can pass the Canine Good Citizen® Test.

• To pass the test, practice many times before it's taken.

• The handler should be relaxed during the test.

A canine good citizen makes a great neighbor and family pet.

Part 3

Solving Problems

Like people, dogs can develop a variety of habits that become problems for those that live with them. Happily, though, when it comes to dogs, the dog owner can solve most of the problems and if not, professional help is available.

Here, some of the more common problems are addressed, along with tips on how to deal with them.

Car Sickness

Some puppies will get sick in a car and some will not. If your pup gets carsick, there are usually two reasons for it. First, it may be caused by motion sickness, or second, by fear—riding in a big, scary machine can have calamitous effects on a puppy's digestive

Some dogs get carsick easily.

Make car rides a pleasant experience for your dog.

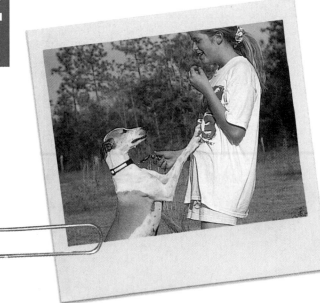

system. The fear may be related to an experience in the dog's early puppyhood; perhaps she remembers that a car took her away from her mother or to the vet for vaccinations.

To treat the fear, acclimate your puppy with a gentle introduction to the vehicle. First, sit in the parked car and hold the puppy in your lap. While her eyes are flitting around and her stomach flitting a little too, she has a security blanket—you. Praise, pet, and soothe her, and when she gets out, give her a little treat.

If she is small enough, put some newspaper on the floor and feed her. When she is finished, take her out and praise her.

Another way to get her used to the vehicle is to place her a carrier and run the vehicle for ten minutes or so in your driveway, repeating this procedure every day for one week. Of course, make sure that there is adequate ventilation for you and the puppy.

If the carsickness continues, the problem may be motion sickness. The solution is to visit your vet, who will be able to dispense a variety of medications to treat the problem.

Jumping Up

Most puppies are naturally friendly and rambunctious, and jumping up on people can be part of this rambunctious behavior. This may be disregarded or even welcomed by some people when a puppy is small, but it will not be appreciated if the puppy keeps the habit as it grows to maturity, especially if the puppy becomes a large dog. Any dog, no matter what size, can have muddy paws or injure someone, especially the elderly or small children.

The solution is to train the dog not to jump when you're pretty sure she will, such as when a family member comes home. Catching her in the act is the only way to stop the behavior.

First, slip on the leash and training collar. Grab the leash about two feet from the collar and make sure there's some slack. Then, when the dog jumps, give the leash a quick sideways tug (not straight back or you can choke her) and say, "No!"

Pulling on the leash will make her feet hit the ground, and as soon as they do, praise her. As soon as she's off, give the sit command, and then praise her some more. Teach her to sit every time someone comes in, and praise her and give her a treat when she obeys.

Do not allow bad habits to form in your household.

Jumping Up on Furniture

Jumping up on furniture can be another problem for a puppy, and you may inadvertently cause it yourself. If you sit down on the couch and then beckon to the pup to vault into your lap, you are encouraging the practice. The piece of furniture still will be there when your lap isn't, and the puppy will not be able to tell the difference. Your best bet is to prevent bad habits from forming in the first place. If you do not want your puppy on the furniture, never allow her on it. If you allow her some times and not others, she will be confused.

If you are in the room at the time the puppy is jumping up, issue negative verbal commands in a stern voice, as you would with any other training procedure. The puppy will get the idea. If she doesn't respond, lift her off at the same time you issue the command.

Be consistent with household rules.

Part 3

All puppies need to chew physically and developmentally.

Part 3

Chewing

Like babies, puppies chew on things to help their new teeth come in, but unlike babies, puppies have the physical wherewithal to gnaw on furniture or destroy your belongings. As with the puppy jumping on the furniture, reprimand her when you catch her in the act. Prevention is the key to keeping your puppy and your belongings safe. If you cannot supervise your puppy, put her in a safe place, like a gated area or her crate so that she cannot get into trouble. Be sure to provide her with plenty of safe chewing alternatives, such as a Nylabone™, to keep her mouth occupied.

You also can discourage the chewing behavior by sprinkling a variety of substances, such as tabasco sauce, cayenne pepper, or bitter spray on the furniture where she's likely to launch the assault.

Fear of Noise

Noise is upsetting to everyone, including dogs. It has been linked to a variety of maladies, including high blood pressure, anxiety, and cardiovascular disease, as well as damage to the ears, as documented among many rock musicians. Some breeds, such as hunting dogs, are naturally noise shy, and they may be afraid of outbursts of noise such as firecrackers, thunderclaps, or the blaring or a horn (the same things that make us cringe!). Before you know it, your dog may be cowering under a bed or in a closet and getting there is likely to be done at high speed with no regard for what's in her way.

Home Alone

A couple of surveys of dog owners indicate that it's not a good idea to leave a dog home alone— either for the owner or dog. The following facts emerged:

- 42 percent of dog owners interviewed felt stress when they could not find someone to care for their dogs while at work.

- 68 percent of the dog owners interviewed said that they have returned home late and have discovered that their dogs have had "accidents."

- 97 percent of owners say that letting their dogs outside and providing safe area outside is very important.

- 95 percent of owners believe it's important to create a sense of freedom for their dog.

It is possible to train a dog to ignore a noise. The key to calming a dog is to acclimatize her to it from the beginning. The worst thing you can do is to show the dog that you're afraid of noise. Rather, you should try to link it to a pleasant experiences. If a noise occurs, give the dog a treat. If you ignore it, your dog will learn to ignore it as well.

Aggression

If a puppy shows signs of aggression, such as growling or biting, this is not something to be taken lightly. You should never let a puppy do something that would be unacceptable for an adult dog to do. Any sign of aggression or dominant behavior should be dealt with right away, because it will be far less humorous when a dog is full grown and growling at you.

One thing that you should not do is shower an aggressive dog with love, figuring that it might

Put your dog in a safe place when he can't be supervised.

One vet reports that a kennel who trained hunting dogs would go a little overboard to acclimate the dogs to loud noises. At feeding time, as his dogs ate, he would pound metal pans and create a ruckus—a commotion that could be heard quite a distance away. As a result, the dogs he trained could have stood calmly in the middle of a firing range. Of course, if you're trying to do this in a populated area your neighbors may want you on the firing range— as a target!

Distract your dog with toys and praise if he seems fearful.

Part 3

Aggressive behavior is unacceptable in a family pet.

If your dog is behaving unusually, visit your veterinarian.

have been abused when very young. Your dog will interpret any positive feedback for the aggression as your approval of it.

Also, if the dog is aggressive toward you, don't be aggressive back. Your aggression is a challenge to the dog, and she will respond with more aggression.

The best procedure is a two-part approach. First, bring the problem to the attention of your veterinarian. The doctor can check the dog out to make sure that the aggression doesn't have a physical cause. If the dog is on medication, for example, this might cause the problem, or your dog may be experiencing some pain or illness that is changing her behavior.

If the vet doesn't find anything, the next step is to get a professional dog trainer familiar with aggression problems to look into it.

In some cases, aggression can have a very unhappy ending for you and the dog. But that unhappy ending can be far less worrisome than what can happen if a full-grown, aggressive dog is roaming around.

Chasing Cars and Bikes

This problem can start emerging in late puppyhood or adolescence when the herding or protective instinct that a dog has kicks in. The dog is trying to round up the moving car or bicycle, and it's something the animal should be cured of quickly. If the dog isn't corrected, this behavior can be much more difficult to control and may result in accident that can seriously injure the dog or a driver.

There are a variety of exercises used to correct the behavior, and although some may seem a bit harsh, they surely beat the

Old Age and Health

Your dog can't speak, so you are the best judge of whether she is evincing changes that may indicate a medical problem. Behavioral changes may be a direct result of a medical problem. Veterinarians say it's a good idea to screen a dog for aging problems when she has reached the time when the particular breed is considered senior. When the dog is older, you should bring her to the vet twice a year.

There are variations, but in general, dogs that are the following weights should be screened at the prescribed times:

If the dog is over 80 pounds, screen for old age symptoms between 4 and 6 years of age; if she is 51 to 80 pounds, screen between 6 and 8 years of age; if she is 16 to 50 pounds, screen between 7 and 9 years of age; and 15 pounds or less, begin to screen between 9 and 11 years of age.

alternative. The simplest way to stop a dog from chasing a bicyclist or car is to yell, "No!" several times when the dog takes off. If she has been trained, she'll understand the command, particularly in the tone of voice you deliver it in. If this doesn't work, escalate the corrections. If the dog starts to bolt after a car, take out your noisemaker, make a very loud noise, and yell "No!" This should startle the dog into stopping before she runs.

Dog trainer Bash Dibra said he cured one dog of car chasing by letting a friend drive down the street, and allowing the dog to chase after the car. When the dog caught up to the car, his friend yelled "No!" and threw a balloon filled with water in the dog's face. After a couple of times, the dog stopped.

Barking

Though it's not bad for a dog to bark sometimes, particularly when a stranger comes onto your property, some dogs bark at anything they see—a squirrel, a bird, a moving train, anything. This type of dog may bark until you and your neighbors are ready to go bananas.

A fenced-in yard will deter your dog from chasing cars or bicycles.

Problem behavior can be a result of boredom.

Keep your dog leashed at all times to avoid confrontations with other dogs.

Here, again, the noisemaker–a can with coins, your keys, or a chain–comes into play. Just toss it down and say, "No!" when your dog barks. Don't forget to praise her when the barking stops. Stop the dog every time she starts to bark, and eventually, she'll quiet down.

Fighting

Years ago, when I was in the Army and standing at attention with a bunch of other soldiers, two dogs started to fight, totally disrupting our concentration. A very brave Airborne Ranger tried to stop the fight by pulling their snapping mouths apart with his gloved hands–but no luck. Then, a Sergeant who obviously was experienced in breaking up dog fights ambled over, grabbed each dog by its tail and pulled them apart. The fight ended.

This still strikes me as a good way to break up a dog fight, but if the dogs are very large, you may not want to venture in. If you are reluctant to grab a dog by the tail, you can at least try to minimize damage. If there are other dogs in the area, move them away so they don't get involved in the violence. Another good way to break up the fight is to toss water or turn a hose on them.

Do whatever you can do to break up the fight as quickly as possible. The longer it goes on, the more likely it is that one of the dogs will suffer serious damage.

Key Points
• Catching your dog in the act is the only way to correct problem behavior.

Part 3

If you see a dog approach you as you walk with your dog, don't tighten up on the lead. This will give your dog a protective signal and your dog may go into an aggressive mode.

Rather, keep the lead loose, and give the dog a series of commands to heel to help her avoid eye contact with the other dog. Eye contact usually precedes hostilities.

A well-socialized dog will make friends easily.

• Do not allow bad habits to form in the first place. For example, if you do not want your puppy on the furniture, never allow her on it. If you allow her on it some times and not other times, she will be confused.

• Prevention is the key to keeping your puppy and your belongings safe. If you cannot supervise your puppy, put her in a safe place, like a gated area or her crate so that she cannot get into any trouble.

• You should never let a puppy do something that would be unacceptable for an adult dog to do.

• If your dog starts to display problems, especially after training, take her to the veterinarian. There may be a medical cause for the behavior.

Part 3

Part Four
Advanced Training

"Still teaching your dog simple tricks like 'roll over' and 'play dead,' Simmons?"

11

Off-Leash Training

The ability to control your dog without a leash is a great advantage to both you and the dog. It can allow the dog to run frcc in safc arcas, and you are assured that when you want him to obey you, he will.

Of course, there are people who never take their dogs out of the confines of their property and may think that off-leash training is not that important. However, a friend of mine named Jim provided a perfect example of the benefits of off-leash training.

Jim owned a Labrador Retriever that used to roam his yard. Whenever Jim took him for walks, he was on a leash. One day, when Jim and his dog were downtown, a squirrel seemed to materialize out of

Once he knows the basic commands, your dog is ready for off-leash training.

nowhere. The Lab bolted, pulling the leash from my friend's hand.

The squirrel beat a hasty retreat across the street, which had its fair share of traffic, and my friend screamed for the dog to stop–to no avail. The Lab was almost clipped by a car twice, and the second time, the dog was only inches from the front fender, a heartbeat–Jim's heartbeat–away from injury or death.

After recovering the dog, my friend literally started to cry, and the very next day he started to inquire into off-leash training.

There are other good reasons to train your dog off-leash. You can control the dog when guests are in the house, you can have a high degree of control when you're in the house, and you will have a trustworthy dog when you are out in the neighborhood.

Off-leash training should be done in a quiet, safe area.

Saving a Life

Dog expert Gina Spadafori reported one of the best examples of the value of training. "I was camping with some friends along with Lance, an obedience-titled dog of no small accomplishments and, by far, the best-trained dog I've ever owned. Lance had wandered across a small dirt road in the campground to put his mark on some shrubbery and was ambling back when some idiot in a pickup truck came blasting down the road. Three more steps and Lance would have been toast, but instead of calling him, I shouted, "Down!" and he dropped where he stood. It was five full minutes before my heart started beating normally again, but Lance was safe.... A better testimony of the importance of training I have yet to run across."

One caution: If training fails, it's usually during the off-leash phase. It's very important to be sure that your dog is ready for it. He should obey commands reliably while on his leash. If you sense that he's not ready, go back to on-leash work before returning to off-leash exercises.

The Basics

When you train a dog off leash, caution is the name of

Part 4

the game. The training should be done in a place where the dog can't get hurt if he decides to bolt off somewhere on his own. A fenced-in yard or a large field would be ideal.

Distractions are your major concern while training off leash, and these may be so strong that the dog won't respond to your commands. In order to get his attention, you must apply a stronger distraction.

The key to getting and keeping your dog's attention is noise. A dog's hearing is second only to his sense of smell, and you can startle him into refocusing by making appropriate noise at the right time.

Toys can help keep your dog's attention on you.

There are a number of things that make good distractions. A soda can or a tin box with a dozen pennies in it and the opening taped shut makes a good noise and gets the dog's attention. When this is tossed to the ground or shaken, it makes quite a racket. The dog is sure to be distracted from his other distraction and give you his undivided attention.

Another device is a "throw chain." These are simply chains linked together to give them some bulk. When they're tossed on the ground, they make a sharp metallic sound. You can buy a throw chain in pet stores or buy a chain collar about three feet long and tie a couple of knots in it to give it bulk.

Use a specific noise or signal to get your dog's attention.

The ring of keys in your pocket is another useful device. (Remember, noise is "key.") Flip these on the ground and they will make a sound sufficient enough to startle your dog and get his attention.

Loosen the leash gradually until your dog is performing reliably.

You can also get the attention of your dog by running away from him. This takes advantage of the dog's vision, which is very good at spotting something in motion. To get his attention, wave your arms and start running away from him. The dog will be able to see you and will follow his basic instinct to chase–in this case, you. As he gets closer, slow down. When he is close enough to you, pet and praise him for his behavior.

Once the dog gets used to the distraction, he'll get to know it, and then just a little noise will turn his attention toward you.

Clapping your hands or smacking your thigh may also be effective. As my friend, trainer Captain Haggerty, says, "Whatever works."

Loosening the Leash

To get your dog to follow off-leash commands, he needs to perform the exercises gradually. The leash should be loosened and gradually removed as he gets more reliable in his commands.

First, attach a regular six-foot leash to a training collar on the dog. He will be on your left because, as mentioned earlier, all training should occur with the dog on the handler's left. You want the dog to know that the leash is loose (and he will). After attaching the leash to the dog, run the end or handle over the back of your neck and let it hang down so the end is within arm's reach if the dog's decides to bolt.

Go through the basic on-leash commands of heel, sit, and stay as you walk with the dog, but don't

Keep the leash with reaching distance while performing the commands.

make him walk a straight line. Turn left and right or perhaps do a figure eight, a circle, or parallelogram! Get the dog moving, and be ready to grab the leash.

If the dog bolts, you can grab and snap the leash to correct him, or better yet, use your noisemaker. Don't forget to praise the dog when he does the exercise.

Practice heel, sit, and stay for ten minutes or until you feel the dog is doing well with the leash loose. If he doesn't do an exercise correctly, start again from scratch.

Getting Even Looser

The next step is to make the leash even looser. First, tell the dog to stay, and then extend the leash out fully toward you on the ground, with the handle within a few inches of your foot. It should be close enough so you can step on it and restrain the dog if you have to. In other words, there's six feet between you and the dog, but the end of the leash is right there for control.

With the leash still lying on the ground, command the dog to go down, stay, sit, come, and finally heel. As he completes these exercises, don't forget to praise him vociferously. A dog responding positively while training is a great feeling for the trainer.

At some point during these commands, the dog may try to take off. It's important to give him a correction right away—grab or step on the leash, snap it, and say, "No!" Use your noisemaker and then make the dog heel. You should wait a couple of minutes before starting the exercise again.

Having an energized and positive attitude is conducive to training.

Correct your dog by getting his attention and trying the exercise again.

Repetition will ensure that your dog retains his training.

When your dog obeys consistently, allow him to go off leash in a safe area.

Do these exercises until the dog does them well, then connect the dog to a retractable long leash that is 26 feet long and practice the exercises from short distances. Gradually increase the length of the leash until the dog is doing exercises 26 feet from you.

When the dog has done well with looser and longer leashes, he's just about ready to go off leash. Before you take the leash off, it's a good idea to double check to make sure he's ready.

There are a couple of ways to do this. One is to have the dog follow the commands you give using a thin, breakable 12-inch piece of string attached to the dog's collar and snap ring on the leash. If the dog can perform the exercises without snapping the string, he's ready for the big time. If he breaks the string, then you should start the exercises from scratch.

Another good exercise to double check a dog's off-leash readiness for exercises is to feed one end of a four-foot string under his collar and pull it through until the ends are even. Then take the dog through the various commands. If the dog bolts, grab the rope and start the exercises all over again. Going through everything again may seem tedious, but a dog has a short-term memory. Repetition will ensure that your dog retains the information.

Distractions
When you feel your dog is trained well enough, you can take him off the leash, but it's important to try to distract the dog while you train. Imitate the outside world by filling your training area with kids,

other dogs, and other animals. Don't hold back! If such things distract the dog, they'll be doing it where he's safe.

If your dog can obey with all these distractions, he's ready to do it anywhere. However, you should always be alert to the fact that your dog may possibly revert to his basic instincts when off leash. Be aware of his body language so you can prevent a problem before it starts, and carry around your noisemaker to distract him. For example, if your dog suddenly stiffens when he spots a squirrel, get ready to restrain him.

Key Points

• A dog must be able to perform the basic exercises before he can do off-leash exercises.

• A dog should be weaned away from the leash gradually before performing completely free of it.

• Dogs are subject to many distractions outside. Your best bet is to train him in a safe place where distractions are present to get him used to them.

• Getting your dog's attention with noisemakers, such as a can with pennies in it, can aid greatly in refocusing a dog's attention on the trainer.

• If a dog fails one part of a command, it's best to start over again.

• Before letting a dog train off-leash, use double checks to test his reliability.

The ability to control your dog off leash is important to his safety.

Test your dog's reactions to different distractions.

Part 4

Trick Training

Trick training can be lots of fun, but it all starts with the basics. Before a dog can be trained to do tricks, he must be well trained in the basic obedience commands. Being previously trained creates an environment for new training, and in some cases, the basic commands and tricks are related.

Before trying to train your dog to do any tricks, however, you should evaluate whether or not he's suitable for the job. "Some owners," says a dog trainer friend of mine, "overlook certain things in their desire that their dog be able to do tricks. Some dogs are not physically fit to do the job. They have bad backs or suffer from hip dysphasia or other medical problems."

Before you start training, make sure your dog is physically fit.

Magic Tricks?

We've all been amazed by the incredible sight of a dog doing something that so resembles human behavior that the dog, despite the fact that he has an owner, seems to be doing things on his own.

In fact, dogs do things on command, but in the case of these "show biz" dogs, the commands are very subtle. The owner might raise an eyebrow, tilt a head, or make some other movement, but it is all a dog needs to perform the magical trick.

Dog trainer Bash Dibra describes an example of how this was done with a dog that could seemingly add and subtract. Even the owner didn't claim to understand how the trick was done, and believed that his dog was a genuine genius. By careful observation, Dibra figured out how it was done.

In one phase of this test, the dog would be asked how much a particular numbers added up to, with the answer to be given in the number of barks. For example, the trainer might say, "How much is 5 and 6?" and the dog would bark 11 times. Dibra observed that when the dog completed the correct number of barks, the man inadvertently nodded his head a bit harder and the beginning of a smile showed on his face. The dog interpreted, correctly, that his master was now pleased with him and stopped barking—always just at the right time.

Most dogs can learn how to shake hands.

One owner, he recalls, tried to train his St. Bernard to sit up. It just didn't happen. The dog was too big and ungainly; his high legs could not support his weight. Other owners have been known to try to have their small-sized dogs, such as Chihuahuas, Dachshunds, and Pekingese, jump over walls or through hoops that are like jumping over a building to the dog.

If your dog is well trained and in good health, there's no reason why he can't learn tricks. You may not make him a Hollywood star, but he can be a star in your home. (Then again, he may become a movie star. It happens!) Tricks are like any training: The keys to success are repetition, timely correction, and lavish praise.

Shake Hands

This is a trick that almost all dogs can learn. The dog should be on a leash to start.

Have him sit in front of you, and when he gives you his full attention, say, "Give me your paw" or "Shake hands" and simultaneously tap his right paw and pick it up. The tap and touch will get the dog's attention and focus him to the task, and he should lift his foot reflexively. When he does, praise him.

Repeat the steps a number of times, and as you see the dog getting better and better at it, remove the leash and reduce the taps. Eventually, you will get to the point where the dog can do the trick with just the verbal command.

Once your dog can shake, teach him to wave.

Wave

The success of this trick depends on the dog first having been trained to shake hands. The dog should be sitting facing you. Put out your hand and ask the dog to give him your paw, then put out your hand, palm up. As the dog starts to give you his paw, shake your hand back and forth quickly. Continue to say, "Give me your paw" while the dog continues to wave his paw, trying to make contact with you. When this occurs, say, "Wave" and practice until he can do the trick when you give him the verbal command.

Pick Up and Drop it

To teach this trick, first get an object with which the dog can train. You can use a toy, a Nylabone®, or, even better, a retrieving dummy, an item specifically designed for the exercise, which is available in pet stores.

With the dog on the leash, get down on your haunches. Hold the object near the dog's mouth and say, "Take!" When the dog takes the toy, say, "Hold it." If the dog

Retrieving comes naturally to the sporting breeds.

Some dogs love to swim and will happily retrieve in water.

With the right training, your dog can learn all kind of tricks.

drops the object, say, "No! Hold it!" and place it back in his jaws. Of course, each time he succeeds in holding it, praise him lavishly. Repeat the command as much as necessary.

Once you get a dog to hold an object, the next step is to get him to drop it. After the dog has held the object for five or six seconds, say, "Drop!" and take the item from the dog's mouth, forcing his jaws open if necessary. Repeat the exercise as needed, praising the dog lavishly when he completes the trick.

To embellish the trick, after the dog has picked the object up, make him heel and walk along with the object for some distance before commanding him to drop it. Again, praise him lavishly for a job well done.

Fetch

This trick is dependent on your dog being able to pick up and drop and object with his mouth. Start with the dog on a retractable leash in order to prevent him from running around with the object—which lots of dogs like to do—after he has picked it up.

First, show the dog the item (a ball, bone, toy, or Frisbee™ is good to start with) and when he's focused on it, toss it out to just short of the length of the leash. The dog should scamper for it, and as he does say, "Fetch!" Once he picks it up, say "Bring!" and reel in the leash until the dog is next to you. Then, command him to sit and drop the object.

Once the dog completes the trick successfully, praise him lavishly. Once he has mastered the trick on leash, you can dispense with the leash and get a little trickier, as it were.

Part 4

Place the object at some convenient spot for the dog to reach, for example, at the end of a driveway or in a backyard, and make a throwing motion, at the same time uttering, "Fetch!" When the dog reaches the object, say "Bring!" and when he brings it back, say, "Drop!" Once you have the object in your hand, praise the dog exuberantly.

As you might expect, fetching an object will be a lot easier for a Golden Retriever or other hunting dog to master. They didn't get characterized as retrievers for nothing! However, with plenty of practice and praise, any breed of dog can learn this trick.

Speak

When I say that you can teach a dog to "speak," I mean bark, of course. (If your dog can speak in any human language, by all means put a call into Hollywood!)

Barkless Dog

The Basenji is the only dog you'll have real trouble teaching how to speak, because as the "Barkless Dog," he doesn't bark.

For this trick, you need a favorite snack as a reward, for example, a square of liver or piece of cheese. Hold the tidbit in your hand and move the treat around as you say, "Speak." The vast majority of dogs will bark. When he does, you should give him the tidbit, praising him at the same time.

Some dogs will be shy. If this is the case, hold the treat as suggested, but get a little crazy with your physical motions. Try jumping up and down or waving an arm until the dog barks, then quickly let him have the treat and praise him.

Roll Over

The roll over is another easy trick to teach any dog; however, be careful–the dog should not have spine or joint problems.

To do the trick, the dog must first know the down command, and it is necessary for him to wear a leash. It also requires a little extra motivation–a tasty tidbit does the trick. Hold the tidbit in your

Teach your dog the down command before he rolls over.

Part 4

A treat held over his head will encourage your dog to sit up or dance.

left hand and have the dog go into the down position. Hold the tidbit close to the dog's nose, and then take a step to your right and say, "Roll over." Make a circular motion with your hand to indicate the rolling action, or if your dog doesn't get it, physically move the dog. Take another step to the right and repeat the command. Once the dog does the trick, give him the tidbit and praise lavishly.

Dance

This is a trick that certain large breeds may not be able to perform, because it involves them standing on their hind legs. Also, some dogs may not be able to do it because they're too young and have not yet developed enough muscle power. Usually, small dogs such as terriers, toy dogs, and Poodles do it very well. I had one friend who owned a Chihuahua who was very entertaining; he could dance so well, he looked almost human.

Have the dog sit in front of you with a leash on. Hold a tasty tidbit above his head so that he lifts his head. Then gently pull the leash up so that he gradually stands on his hind legs, urging him with the command, "Up, dance!" As soon as the dog gets on his hind legs, pull the leash so it makes a circle, and then give him the treat and praise. Repeat the trick until he can do it without the leash.

Sit Up

This is a trick that also may be too difficult for some dogs to do because of physical limitations. On the other hand, terrier breeds such as Westies, Bostons, and Cairns are particularly good at it.

Before you begin training, it's a good idea to test the dog's physical limitations. To do this, first put on his leash, and then pull the dog straight up until he is sitting on his haunches and see if he can hold the position for a few seconds. If he holds the position, he can do the trick and give him a treat and praise.

Part 4

Start by having the dog sit in front of you while on his leash. Begin pulling the dog up with the leash while saying, "Sit up," then drop the leash and stand back. If the dog stays up, praise him highly; if not, repeat the command until the trick is mastered. If necessary, you can also hold his paws up and say, "Stay!"

Jumping

The key to this trick is to do it gradually. Don't expect your pet to jump over your head on the first day that you train him. Here, again, knowledge of the basic commands, in this case the ability to heel, is required. Also, take your dog's size and stature into consideration before teaching him to jump over any obstacle. Obviously a Dachshund will never be able to clear a five-foot jump, no matter how well trained he is.

First, set up a low stick hurdle by placing some vertical sticks with one laid across them horizontally or a pair of pillows with a stick across it on the grass. With your dog on a leash, make the dog heel and have him step over the hurdle as you say "Up!" or "Over!" Once he steps over the hurdle, command him to sit and praise him lavishly.

Next, stand next to one of the verticals on the hurdle with the horizontal bar clear and encourage the dog to go over, commanding, "Up!" or "Over!" Once he does it, praise him lavishly. Then, using a retractable leash, have the dog sit on one side of the hurdle while you stand on the other. Using the leash to urge him over, give him the "Up" or "Over" command until he does it, then praise.

Jumping should be taught only to dogs in the best condition.

Teach your dog to jump if you plan to compete in agility.

Part 4

Once he does it, move both the dog and yourself further and further from the hurdle, with you on one side and the dog on the other, and repeat the trick.

When you are confident the dog can jump without the leash, remove it and command him to jump. How high you train the dog to jump will depend on the dog: some breeds can jump shoulder height. However, training a dog to jump should be done slowly over a period time, and always keep in mind that every time he lands on his feet, it causes stress on his entire body.

Crawling

This command is, of course, one of the staples in the motion picture business, and is one of the oddest things to see a dog do, therefore one of the more satisfying tricks to teach.

You should start training for the trick with the dog in the down position. Place one of your hands on the dog's shoulders and hold a tasty tidbit close to his nose. Keeping your hand in place, tell the dog to crawl. If he tries to get up, keep a little pressure on his shoulders so that he knows you want him to stay down. When the dog has done one step crawling, praise him and repeat until the dog can do one step without any help and starts to grasp what the "crawl" command is all about. When he can do this, repeat the procedure until he can do several steps, then give him the same command from a standing position, rather than a down position.

Your dog should know basic obedience before you try to teach him any tricks.

Back Up

This is another great movie trick. We've all seen dogs backing up in the face of various types of threats with a decidedly fearful, perhaps snarling facial expression.

The trick is not difficult to master. Start with the dog standing in front of you and issue the command, "Back up" as you start toward the dog. When the dog backs up, praise him, and then continue practicing the exercise. Eventually, when the dog is doing the trick very easily, tell him to "Back

Part 4

up" without going toward him. Praise the dog as before, and repeat the exercise.

Key Points

• Before trying to train a dog to do specialized tricks, he should be obedience trained so that he is more amenable to this advanced training.

• Make sure the dog is physically able to perform the tricks.

• Every time a dog does a trick that involves great physical effort, it is stressful for his body.

Special Training

As a dog owner and trainer, you may want to take your dog to another level when it comes to training. You'll be happy to know that there are a variety of dog sports and organized activities available to expand your horizons. Also, for those who are so inclined, there are ways to train your dog to make a difference–sometimes a big difference–in someone else's life.

The following brief list of some of the kinds of things that are out there for you and your dog to do together–all dogs, young, old, purebred, and mixed breed, are welcome.

Which Activity for You?

Just as you would be wise to evaluate your own

Advanced training should be fun and rewarding for both dog and owner.

Many organizations sponsor obedience trials.

There are several obedience titles that your dog can earn.

skills and innate abilities if you were to enter a competition, so too should you evaluate your dog to see what he'd be best suited for. For example, your Bloodhound probably wouldn't be interested in flyball competition, and your Chihuahua would look pretty silly competing in Schutzhund.

After you decide what you want to do, you can seek out people who can clue you in on training classes or clubs. To find these folks, you can surf the Internet, contact your national dog registries or take a trek to the library to find books and magazines. Before you know it, you'll be hooked up with the right people and on your way to having fun with your dog.

Obedience

Years ago, only purebred dogs competed in obedience, but that is no longer true. Today, mixed breeds, older dogs, and younger dogs are welcome to participate. Many organizations, including the American Kennel Club (AKC), United Kennel Club (UKC), and Canadian Kennel Club (CKC) sponsor these events. However, each of these organizations has its own rules and regulations, and you should contact them to get the information you need to get involved.

The obedience test sponsored by the AKC has three levels of achievement: Novice, Open, and Utility. The dog starts with a perfect score, in this case 200, and then does the various exercises, while the examiner subtracts points when the dog makes an error. If the handler has to repeat a command twice, the dog is disqualified.

These obedience tests are not easy. It takes an average of two to three years to attain a degree in each class. Once the dog attains his degree, he competes with other dogs for overall championships, with points being awarded for first and second place finishes in the two highest classes, and the value of the win decided by how many dogs are in each class.

If you are contemplating entering your dog in an obedience competition, make no mistake: These competitions are intense and often decided by extremely close scores. Your dog must be well trained to excel.

Search and Rescue

Some dogs are wonderful at rescuing people. It is not uncommon for a St. Bernard is able to detect heat coming off a person who's buried in deep snow. It is a small wonder that they are called on when someone is missing on a snowy mountainside. The German Shepherd is also ideal for this type of work. It is strong breed, his coat is insulated against cold, and he is very smart; he takes to training like a duck to water.

This search and rescue Lab looks for an avalanche victim.

Training for search and rescue work starts in puppyhood. All the commands are done off leash, so this skill is developed, as well as agility and strength, because search and rescue dogs must often go into areas that are dangerous to traverse.

The handler, of course, must also be trained and when both dog and man are ready, they can join a team or organization that specializes in this kind of work.

Earthdog Trials

Earthdog trials are for the "go-to-ground" terriers (the smaller terriers and Dachshunds) that were originally bred to go into dens and tunnels after prey, which consisted of all types of small varmints, from rats to badgers. There are four class levels at a licensed test: Introduction to Quarry (for beginning handlers and dogs); Junior Earthdog; Senior Earthdog; and Master Earthdog. The object of the test is to give your dog an opportunity to display his ability to follow game and to "work" the quarry. They "work" by showing interest in the game by barking, digging, and scratching. The quarry can either be two adult rats, which must be caged to be protected from the dogs, or artificial quarry that is located

Field trials are designed to test the abilities of the sporting breeds.

behind a barrier, properly scented, and capable of movement. The dogs eligible to participate in Earthdog trials are Dachshunds and Australian, Bedlington, Border, Cairn, Dandie Dinmont, Fox (Smooth and Wire), Lakeland, Norfolk, Norwich, Scottish, Sealyham, Silky, Skye, Welsh, and West Highland White Terriers.

Field Trials

These tests are designed to test the mettle of hunting dogs. There is a specific test for each breed:

Beagling–Currently, there are three types of trials: Brace, the oldest, is run in braces of two or three dogs that are judged primarily on their accuracy trailing a rabbit; Small Pack Option (SPO), which divides the dogs into packs of seven to pursue rabbits; and Large Pack, which turn all the dogs in the class loose to find and track hares.

Basset Hounds and Dachshunds–These trials are run in a similar fashion as the Beagle Brace trials, but are held separately.

Pointing Breeds–The AKC offers pointing breed field trials and hunting tests. The dogs are run in braces around a course on which birds are released so that they can demonstrate their ability to find birds, point, and retrieve the downed birds.

The eligible pointing breeds are the Brittany, English Setter, German Shorthaired Pointer, Pointer, Gordon Setter, Irish Setter, Vizsla, Weimaraner, and Wirehaired Pointing Griffon.

Retrievers are tested on their ability to find game and return it to their owner.

Retrievers–Retrievers are tested on their ability to remember or "mark" the location of downed birds and to return the birds to their handlers. Both the hunting tests and the field trials have different levels of difficulty, requiring dogs to mark multiple birds and find unmarked birds, called blind retrieves.

The breeds that are eligible for these trials are the Chesapeake, Curly-Coated, Flat Coated, Golden, and Labrador Retrievers, and the Irish Water Spaniel.

Spaniels–Spaniels are judged on their natural and trained ability to hunt, flush, and retrieve game on both land and water. Breeds that are eligible for hunting tests are the Clumber, Cocker, English Cocker, English Springer, Sussex, and Welsh Springer Spaniels; presently, only Cocker, English Cocker, and English Springer Spaniels are eligible to compete in field trials.

Tracking allows your dog to use his nose in the performance ring.

Tracking

All dogs love to use their noses; they use them to communicate with people and other dogs every day. Tracking trials allow dogs to demonstrate their natural ability to recognize and follow scent. This vigorous outdoor activity is especially great for those canine athletes that have an inherent affinity for tracking, like dogs that are in the Hound Group.

There are three titles that a dog can earn in tracking events. The first level is called the TD or Tracking Dog title. A dog can earn his TD by following a track laid down by a human from 30 minutes to 2 hours before. The rules describe certain turns in a 440- to 500-yard track. The second title, TDX, or Tracking Dog Excellent, is earned by following an older (laid down 3 to 5 hours before) and a longer (800 to 1,000 yards) track with more turns while overcoming both physical and scenting obstacles. A dog that has

Schutzhund tests the abilities of protection dogs in a controlled setting.

Part 4

Dogs are excellent at providing assistance to the disabled.

A therapy dog offers companionship and brightens the lives of the people he visits.

earned his VST, or Variable Surface Tracking title, has demonstrated his ability to track through urban and wilderness settings by successfully following a three- to five-hour-old track that may take him down a street, through buildings, or through other areas devoid of vegetation.

Schutzhund

Schutzhund is a German term meaning "protection dog," and in this sport, German Shepherds, Rottweilers, Dobermans, and other breeds developed for police work are tested and compete against each other in terms tracking, obedience, and protection.

Therapy Dogs

A number of years ago, some brilliant person got the idea that dogs, because of their essential personalities–sweet, non-judgmental, outgoing, affectionate–might have a positive effect on some humans. Today they are helping to brighten the days of the elderly and sick in hospitals and nursing homes all over the country.

Not every dog is qualified for the job, of course. One can't just go into a pound or pet shelter, get a dog, and present it to someone. Dogs that are selected must have a propensity for the work and must be thoroughly trained. However, the training is worth it, and if you have the right kind of dog and like to see people smile, this may be the work for you.

Herding Trials

These competitions test the dog's ability to herd livestock. In England, herding events involving herding dogs are so popular they're televised, and there was a very popular movie called *Babe* that showed the sheepdog in action.

The following breeds are eligible to compete in herding trials: Australian Cattle Dog, Australian Shepherd, Bearded Collie,

Belgian Malinois, Belgian Sheepdog, Belgian Turvuren, Border Collie, Bouvier des Flandres, Briard, Canaan Dog, Collie, German Shepherd Dog, Old English Sheepdog, Puli, Shetland Sheepdog, Cardigan Welsh Corgi, Pembroke Welsh Corgi, Samoyed, or Rottweiler.

In herding tests, your dog will be judged against a set of standards and can earn advanced titles and championships by competing against other dogs for placements. Livestock used at the trials include sheep, cattle, ducks, or goats. The titles offered are HS (Herding Started), HI (Herding Intermediate), and HX (Herding Excellent). Upon the completion of an HX, a Herding Championship may be earned after accumulating 15 championship points. There are also non-competitive herding clinics and instinct tests given by AKC clubs across the country.

Herding breeds can showcase their talents at herding trials.

Sled Dogs

The International Sled Dog Racing Association is the main authority when it comes to governing sled dog events. A variety of races are run for teams of dogs of all sizes, and not only standard sled dogs, such as Siberian Huskies, can compete. Hounds, Collies, and Poodles may also get into the act.

The events may be run on a carefully prepared snow course, or with no snow. When there is no snow, the sled has wheels, a device known as a gig.

Artic breeds like the Husky have been bred to pull sleds in snowy climates.

Agility

Agility is the fastest-growing dog sport in the US. In agility competitions, the dogs and handlers run an obstacle course against the clock and are judged on speed and their ability to keep on course. In order to compete in agility, both the dog and handler should be in good shape.

Part 4

Agility is thrilling for both the dog and the spectators.

Frisbee™

Frisbee competitions apparently started because a Whippet named Ashley performed gravity-defying feats while catching a flying disc as America watched on television. People were amazed and entranced, and the result is that today there are hundreds of dogs that compete from all over the country in regional events, which culminates in a national finals.

> ### The Iditarod
>
> Probably the most famous sled dog event is the Iditarod, which commemorates the famous run in the middle of these sub-zero nights by brave dogs and men to carry life-saving serum to Nome, Alaska, needed to save the town.

Freestyle

In Freestyle, a handler and a dog follow a carefully choreographed program, set to music and in costume. Just picture you and your dog doing the twist or the mambo–and having lots of fun!

Flyball

This relay competition requires the dog to step on a board that propels a ball into mid-air. The dog must grab the ball then race back across a series of jumps, which he had to jump over to get to the ball-release mechanism in the first place. Once back, another team members take over. This sport is best for athletic dogs that love to play fetch.

Conformation

In conformation shows, breeds compete against one another and are judged on how well they conform to a breed ideal or standard, which represents the best in the breed. Obviously, you need to have a purebred dog that is an outstanding example of the breed to excel at this

This Doberman shows his grace and athleticism at the weave poles.

sport. Being part of a conformation competition can be expensive and difficult, but thousands of people love it, and one never knows how one will do.

There are six different regular classes in which dogs may be entered. The following classes are offered to male and female dogs separately in each breed entered at the show. Once the dog is a champion, it can compete for Best of Breed without having to win in the other classes.

Puppy Class–Open to six- to nine- or nine- to twelve-month-old dogs that are not yet champions.

Twelve to Eighteen Months–Open to 12- to 18-month-old dogs that are not yet champions.

Novice–Open to dogs that have never won a blue ribbon in any of the other classes or that have won less than three ribbons in the novice class.

Bred by Exhibitor–Open to dogs that have been bred by the same person that is exhibiting them.

American Bred–Open to dogs whose parents were mated in America and that were born in America.

Open–Open to any dog of that breed.

In conformation, your dog is judged against the standard of the breed.

After these classes are judged, all the dogs that won first place in the classes compete again to determine which dog is the best of the winning dogs. This is also done separately for male and female dogs. Only the best male (Winners Dog) and the best female (Winners Bitch) receive championship points. A Reserve Winner award is given in each sex to the runner up. The Winners Dog and the Winners Bitch then go onto compete with the champions for the title of Best of Breed. At the end of the Best of Breed competition, three awards are usually given. Best of Breed is given to the dog judged best in its breed category. Best of Winners is given to the dog judged as best between the Winners Dog and the Winners Bitch, and Best of Opposite Sex

Part 4

is given to the best dog that is the opposite sex of the Best of Breed winner.

Only the Best of Breed winners advance to compete in the group competition (each breed falls into one of seven group classifications). Four placements are awarded in each group, but only the first place winner advances to the Best in Show competition.

Training your dog for competition can help build a bond between you.

Dog showing can be a very rewarding experience, but be careful–once bitten by the show bug, many people get addicted!

Key Points

• Evaluate both your skills and your dog's skills before choosing an event or activity.

• Seek out people to mentor and help you become involved.

• Have fun!

Part 4

Resources

Tracking Information
Getting Started in Obedience and Tracking and
Obedience and Tracking Regulations
Published by the American Kennel Club
5580 Centerview Drive
Raleigh, NC 27606-3390
919-233-9767 (Customer service number)

The American Rescue Dog Association
PO Box 151
Chester, NY 10918
www.ardainc.org

National Association for Search and Rescue
4500 Southgate Place, Suite 100
Chantilly, VA 22021
www.nasar.org

Getting Started in Performance Events–Earthdog Tests
Published by the American Kennel Club
5580 Centerview Drive
Raleigh, NC 27606-3390
919-233-9767 (Customer service number)

The American Working Terrier Association
503 NC 55 West
Mt. Olive, NC 28465
919-658-0929

The Association of Pet Dog Trainers (APDT)
17000 Commerce Parkway, Suite C
Mt. Laurel, NJ 08054
1-800-PET-DOGS
information@apdt.com

Hunting Test Herald, Getting Started in Field Events, and Pointing Breed Field Trial News
Published by the American Kennel Club
5580 Centerview Drive
Raleigh, NC 27606-3390
919-233-9767 (Customer service number)

Delta Society
289 Perimeter Road E.
Renton, VA 98055-1329
800-869-6898
www2.deltasociety.org/deltasociety/

Therapy Dogs Inc.
PO Box 2786
Cheyenne, WY 82003
307-638-3223
homt.ptd.net/~compudog.tdi.html

Therapy Dogs International
00 Dartley Road
Flandres, NJ 07836

Canine Companions for Independence
PO Box 446
Santa Rosa, CA 95402-0446

Dogs for the Deaf
10175 Wheeler Road
Central Point, OR 97502
541-826-9220

Rules and Regulations for Herding Tests and Herding Trials
Published by the American Kennel Club
5580 Centerview Drive
Raleigh, NC 27606-3390
919-233-9767 (Customer service number)

United States Border Collie Handler's Association
2915 Anderson Lane
Crawford, TX 76638
254-486-2500

North American Sheep Dog Society
Route 3
McLeansboro, IL 62859

Australian Shepherd Club of America
E. SH 21
Bryan, TX 77808
409-778-1082
www.asca.org

North American Dog Agility Council
HRC 2, Box 277
St. Maries, ID 83861
www.teleport.com/~jhglund.nadachom.htm

United States Dog Agility Association
PO Box 850955
Richardson TX 75085-0955
214-231-9700
www.usdaa.com

Index

Photo Credits

Larry Allen: p. 171, bottom; p. 211, top.

Paulette Braun: p. 46; p. 48, bottom; p. 66, bottom; p. 76; p. 86, top; p. 112; p. 119, bottom; p. 135, bottom; p. 136, bottom; p. 196; p. 201, bottom.

Tara Darling: p. 77; p. 208, top.

Isabelle Francais: p. 11; p. 18; p. 19; p. 20; p. 21; p. 22; p. 23; p. 25; p. 26; p. 27; p. 29; p. 30; p. 31; p. 33, top; p. 37; p. 42; p. 43; p. 44; p. 45; p. 47; p. 48, top; p. 49; p. 50; p. 51; p. 52; p. 53; p. 54; p. 56; p. 57; p. 59; p. 61; p. 62; p. 63; p. 64; p. 65; p. 66, top; p. 67; p. 69; p. 70; p. 71; p. 72; p. 73; p. 74; p. 75; p. 78; p. 79; p. 80; p. 82; p. 84; p. 85; p. 86, bottom; p. 87; p. 91; p. 92; p. 93; p. 94; p. 95; p. 96; p. 97; p. 98; p. 99; p. 100; p. 101; p. 102; p. 105; p. 106; p. 107; p. 108; p. 109; p. 110; p. 111; p. 113; p. 115; p. 116; p. 117; p. 118; p.179, top; p. 121; p. 122; p. 123; p. 124; p. 125; p. 126; p. 127; p. 128; p. 129; p. 130; p. 131; p. 132; p. 134; p. 135, top; p. 136, top; p. 137; p. 138; p. 141; p. 142; p. 143; p. 144; p. 145; p. 146; p. 147; p. 148; p. 149; p. 151; p. 152; p. 155; p. 156; p. 157; p. 158; p. 159; p. 160; p. 161; p. 162; p. 163; p. 165; p. 166; p. 167; p. 168; p. 169, top; p. 170; p. 171, top; p. 172, bottom; p. 173; p. 175; p. 176; p. 177; p. 178; p. 179; p. 180; p. 181; p. 182; p. 183; p. 187; p. 188; p. 189; p. 191; p. 192; p. 193; p. 195; p. 197, top; p. 198; p. 199; p. 200; p. 201, top; p. 202; p. 205; p. 206; p. 208, bottom; p. 209; p. 210; p. 211, bottom; p. 212; p. 213; p. 214.

Connie Isbell: p. 15; p. 33, bottom.

Alan Leschinski: p. 164, top; p.190, bottom.

Liz Palika: p. 164, bottom; p. 169, bottom; p. 172, top; p. 190, top.

Judith Strom: p. 197, bottom; p. 207.

Michael Pifer: Cartoons